DISCOVER THE LOVE
OF YOUR LIFE
ALL OVER AGAIN

THE DIVORCE-PROOFING AMERICA'S MARRIAGES
CAMPAIGN PRESENTS:

DISCOVER THE LOVE
OF YOUR LIFE
ALL OVER AGAIN

BY DR. GARY AND BARBARA ROSBERG

Visit Tyndale's exciting Web site at www.tyndale.com

Discover the Love of Your Life All Over Again

Copyright © 2003 by Gary and Barbara Rosberg. All rights reserved.

Cover photograph copyright © 2003 by Brian MacDonald. All rights reserved.

Authors' photo copyright © 2002 by Thomas and Bruce Photography. All rights reserved.

Designed by Julie Chen

Edited by Linda K. Taylor

Produced with the assistance of The Livingstone Corporation (www.LivingstoneCorp.com).

Published in association with the literary agency of Alive Communications, Inc., 7680 Goddard Street, Suite 200, Colorado Springs, CO 80920.

Unless otherwise indicated, all Scripture quotations are taken from the *Holy Bible,* New Living Translation, copyright © 1996. Used by permission of Tyndale House Publishers, Inc., Wheaton, Illinois 60189. All rights reserved.

All quotations are taken from *Divorce-Proof Your Marriage* by Dr. Gary and Barbara Rosberg, published by Tyndale House, 2002.

ISBN 0-8423-7342-X

Printed in the United States of America

09 08 07 06 05 04 03

7 6 5 4 3 2 1

Dedication

To our nephew
Nathan Warren Bedford
September 21, 1978 – January 4, 2003
You honored Jesus, your wife, daughter, and family
both in life and your homecoming.
And now we honor you.
You guarded your heart and finished strong.

CONTENTS

Introduction

HOW TO USE THIS BOOK

COURSE PURPOSE:
TO LEARN WHAT IT TAKES TO DIVORCE-PROOF YOUR MARRIAGE.

This eight-week workbook course (including a group get-together for a special celebration) was prepared by Gary and Barbara Rosberg as part of a nationwide campaign to keep marriages alive and well. The campaign is called "Divorce-Proofing America's Marriages." This course is designed to help you renew your commitment and love for your spouse. As a result of completing this workbook study together, you will share a deeper resolve to experience God's dream for your marriage, and you will renew your love for each other. You will study six key kinds of love:

- Forgiving love
- Serving love
- Persevering love
- Guarding love
- Celebrating love
- Renewing love

This is the way God loves us, and it is the way we are to love our spouse. Together, you and your spouse will renew your commitment to these six loves, and, in the process, learn to

- forgive offenses,
- serve to meet each other's needs,
- persevere in trials,
- guard against every attack,
- celebrate what makes your marriage unique, and
- renew the bond that will help you feel rooted and connected.

Thus, this course is not just for people who think they're "on the brink." It's for anyone anywhere on the marriage map (as you read about in chapter 2). You don't need to be embarrassed that you're taking this course—as though people will think your marriage must really be in trouble. You may be in a great marriage and you just want to learn how to keep it that way.

You may be starting to feel your "marriage dream" beginning to fade (as we discuss in chapter 1). You want to bring it back to full strength.

You may indeed be in trouble . . . ready to give up . . . feeling that there's no hope left. You will be given the tools that can help you find the strength to keep going and the hope to drive you on.

Wherever your marriage is at, it takes three to make it work—you, your spouse, and God. And that's one powerful combination! We have found, however, that it takes *work* to make a marriage work. The journey into the next few weeks may be a bumpy ride, but we can guarantee that it will be worth it.

Each person will need his/her own copy of this workbook. Each couple will also need a copy of the book *Divorce-Proof Your Marriage* because the weekly assignments include reading chapters from the book. That book is laid out with an introductory part 1 that helps you focus on where your marriage is at right now. Parts 2 through 7 (two chapters each) focus on each of the six kinds of love noted above.

This workbook is designed to equip you to

1. take a realistic look at your marriage and face any difficulty head on;

2. discover the tools needed to strengthen the love in your marriage;

3. learn and practice the types of love that are needed to build a great marriage; and

4. journal your progress on each weekly assignment.

Each week you will meet with your group for some general discussion (don't worry, no baring of your soul or pouring out your heart in front of others). The group discussion is to guide you to think about the topic. Included in the group time is a time for just you and your spouse to talk as well.

The meat of the study, however, comes in the "homework" assignments. After each group lesson you will find three sections for you to work on during the week.

Day One is a time of **Personal Reflection**. Here you will
- Write down how each type of love is experienced in your own life first. Then you'll consider how you are giving and can better give that type of love need to your spouse.
- Determine the godly attitude necessary in your own life to love with these types of love.

Day Two is a time for **Couple Interaction**. Here you will
- Take turns sharing how the different types of love can be met in your life.
- Commit to consistently loving your spouse in those ways.
- Plan a time throughout the week to practice showing those types of love.

Day Three is called **My Assignment**, where you will

- Complete a reading assignment of a few chapters of *Divorce-Proof Your Marriage* by Gary and Barbara Rosberg.
- Plan and practice loving your spouse with the focused kinds of love as discussed in the book.
- Journal your progress by writing down what you did to love in those ways and chronicle your spouse's response.

You are embarking on a marital journey that may very well change the way you love your spouse. Ask God to empower you to be a truly loving husband or wife.

Before the first group session, read *Divorce-Proof Your Marriage*, part 1— chapters 1, 2, and 3. Part of the group discussion will focus on what you read in these first three chapters. Also do the exercises in chapter 2 to help you both determine where your marriage is on the marriage map. Self-tests are available in appendix B.

Group Session One

PURSUE THE DREAM

You should have already read part 1 of the *Divorce-Proof Your Marriage* book. The first three chapters focus on (1) what to do when your dream marriage has become less dreamy; (2) the marriage map; and (3) the dream you can pursue—the fact that you can divorce-proof your marriage.

And make no mistake about it—every marriage needs to be divorce-proofed. Even the best marriages need to be vigilantly guarded. You see, Satan hates happy marriages—and *Christian happy* marriages, well, he despises those! He may not be able to attack you head-on, but in his insidious way, he'll seek to undermine even the best marriage.

So let's begin this journey into discovering the kinds of love you and your spouse can share in order to put up a shield against Satan and keep your marriage strong and secure.

Describe the first time you met your spouse (or your first date). What was it that drew you to him/her?

I saw Jenny in a restaurant with a group of her friends. I thought she was pretty and cute.

When did you know that this person was "the one"?

She was very balanced and had a heart for the Lord. The more I was with her, the more I fell in love with her.

Every engaged couple approaches marriage with expectations, hopes, and dreams. But did you know that God has a dream about marriage? When he planned it way back at the beginning, he designed it to work a particular way. Read Genesis 2:15-25, then answer the questions:

> The Lord God placed the man in the Garden of Eden to tend and care for it.... And the Lord God said, "It is not good for the man to be alone. I will make a companion who will help him." So the Lord God formed from the soil every kind of animal and bird. He brought them to Adam to see what he would call them, and Adam chose a name for each one. He gave names to all the livestock, birds, and wild animals. But still there was no companion suitable for him. So the Lord God caused Adam to fall into a deep sleep. He took one of Adam's ribs and closed up the place from which he had taken it. Then the Lord God made a woman from the rib and brought her to Adam. "At last!" Adam exclaimed. "She is part of my own flesh and bone! She will be called 'woman,' because she was taken out of a man." This explains why a man leaves his father and mother and is joined to his wife, and the two are united into one. Now, although Adam and his wife were both naked, neither of them felt any shame.

1. God designed marriage and has a plan for your marriage. Why did he institute marriage in the first place? Check all that apply.

   ☑ To remove human aloneness
   ❑ To frustrate human beings
   ☑ To encourage human beings
   ❑ To make life perfect
   ❑ To make life difficult
   ❑ To give Adam something to do
   ❑ To populate the earth
   ☑ To meet emotional needs
   ☑ To provide companionship·
   ☑ Other _intamacy_

2. Discuss your answers with the group. Then answer True or False to the following statements:

___F___ The dream marriage is perfect.

___F___ The dream marriage is characterized by an absence of problems.

___F___ The dream marriage means we are always in complete agreement.

___T___ The dream marriage is the fulfillment of God's plan for me and my spouse.

The point is, your dream marriage is indeed possible because

- it doesn't have to be perfect (because it includes two imperfect people);
- it may still have problems (the key is, how you work to solve them);
- it doesn't require complete agreement at all times (need we say more?); and
- it requires an understanding that God put you together in a bond that was part of his dream for you both.

3. In God's plan for marriage, the husband and wife have a relationship character-ized by the words listed below. Place a check mark in the boxes next to words that describe your relationship. Circle the words that describe areas in which you would like to see improvement.

☑ Loving
☑ Compatible
☑ Happy
☑ Permanent
☑ Companions
☑ United in purpose
☑ Emotionally intimate
☐ Emotionally healthy
☑ Growing closer
☑ Content
☑ Spiritually intimate
☐ Honest about faults
☐ Other things that come to mind: _____

Whether your marriage is doing great or could use lots of improvement, you'll both benefit from the types of love Gary and Barb describe in chapter 3.

4. As a group, fill in the blanks below as your leader offers the answers. After filling in the blanks for each section, discuss as a group why this type of love is impor-tant in marriage.

FORGIVING LOVE

Forgiving love offers a *fresh* *start* after you have *offened* and *hurt* each other. Forgiving love equips you to *communicate* on such a *deep* level of acceptance for one another that you can *recover* from the *pain* you occasionally *inflict* on one another and *work* through your offenses. Forgiving love helps you to *reconnect* after you have *hurt* one another.

Every marriage needs forgiving love because
God told us to forgive. Both of us are not perfect.

SERVING LOVE

Serving love helps you *discover* and *meet* each other's deepest *needs*. Serving love is the process of *identifying* needs and taking steps to *meet* them in each other.

Every marriage needs serving love because
there are needs that need to be meet

PERSEVERING LOVE

Persevering love *sustains* you through the *trials* of life. As you implement persevering love in your marriage you will *bond* with your spouse and *enjoy* a love that will *persevre* through your years together.
perserve

Every marriage needs persevering love because
marriage is a long-term life commitment. In order to get through it, you need to be perserving.

GUARDING LOVE *protects*

Guarding love ~~protects~~ your *heart* from *threats* to your marriage. Marriages are *threating* by many forces today. If you are not aware of the *threats* to your marriage, then you are *vulnerable*.

Every marriage needs guarding love because
it's threating and there is an enemy that wants to destroy it.

CELEBRATING LOVE

Celebrating love _equipes_ you to maintain a satisfying _emotional_, _physical_, and _spiritual_ connection. Celebrating love keeps that _spark_ alive, not only in the bedroom but in all areas of the _relationship_. As you learn to celebrate your _oneness_, you will fall in love all over again.

Every marriage needs celebrating love because

you have to balance work with play.

RENEWING LOVE

Renewing love regards the marriage _covenant_ as _unbreakable_. Renewing love _protects_ you from _insecurity_ and provides you with _confident - reassurance_ as you face your future with your spouse.

Every marriage needs renewing love because

to keep things fresh

Gary and Barb say:

As your marriage experiences these six key kinds of love in God's strength, you will be empowered to divorce-proof your marriage. Barb and I are not talking about merely gutting it out in a relationship that is a constant source of agony and unhappiness. That's no dream for marriage; it's a relational nightmare! Rather, we are talking about developing a marriage relationship that results in such a deepened love between you and your spouse that you discover a completeness that could never be attained alone.
(from chapter 3, under heading "A Vision for Divorce-Proofing Your Marriage")

SHARING AS A COUPLE

5. Review the characteristics of marriage in question 3 above. Share with your spouse which ones you felt you were doing well with and which ones you feel you could use some improvement. As your spouse shares, write both categories below. Then compare his/her comments with what you wrote.

WE'RE DOING WELL WITH: WE COULD IMPROVE AT:

PREPARING FOR THE WEEK

As a group, discuss the following five ground rules one by one. After each one is discussed, turn to your spouse to indicate if you are willing to commit to that guideline for this course.

1. **CONCENTRATE ON YOUR SPOUSE'S NEEDS**
   Take the responsibility to "give" to your spouse and trust that God will meet your own needs however he chooses. By being "other focused" and concerned about meeting your spouse's needs first, you may be surprised how God will bless you by involving your spouse in meeting each of your own needs. Will you commit to this with your spouse?
   ☑ Yes ❑ No ❑ Does this mean it's not going to be all about me anymore?

2. **AVOID CRITICISM**
   When it comes time for your spouse to focus on your needs, be careful not to be critical of how he or she hasn't met your past needs. Express how you personally feel without making statements of accusation. Never criticize your spouse to the group. Will you commit to this with your spouse?
   ☑ Yes ❑ No ❑ What happens if I don't?

3. **KEEP YOUR GROUP SHARING TIME SAFE**
   Some, if not all, in your group will want to share the progress that each is making from week to week. Keep your sharing time confidential within your group, and avoid comparing each other's marriage relationships. Make your group a safe place to share your strengths and struggles. Will you commit to this?
   ☑ Yes ❑ No ❑ This means I can't secretly record our group meetings?

4. FOCUS ON "BEING" AS WELL AS "DOING"

Meeting our spouse's needs involves "doing" something. But our "doing" is empowered by our "being" something. As our attitudes are transformed, our behavior changes. So throughout this course you will be asked to focus on certain Christlike attitudes that will direct your actions. Will you ask God to help you change in attitude and action?

☑ Yes ❑ No ❑ I didn't know I needed to be changed.

5. COMPLETE YOUR WEEKLY EXERCISES AND ASSIGNMENTS

You will be asked to spend a couple of hours each week between these group sessions in discovering how to better meet your spouse's needs. Will you commit to at least an hour and a half a week to this course?

☑ Yes ❑ No ❑ Will I get paid?

Now, close in prayer asking God to give each of you the kind of love you need to move your marriage closer to the "dream."

Your assignment for the coming week will be to study the first kind of love called forgiving love. *You will need to read part 2—chapters 4 and 5 in* Divorce-Proof Your Marriage. *Then complete the three days of assignments that follow. It is important to try to complete these three days of assignments at the beginning of the week, so that you have the rest of the week to put into practice forgiving love, which will be discussed in the next group session. The homework assignments are strictly between you and your spouse—so be open and honest as you work separately and then share together this week.*

Week One—Day One

MY PERSONAL REFLECTION:
LEARNING TO FORGIVE

No matter how long ago it was, you probably still remember that moment when you said "I do." Your ceremony may have been simple . . . or sumptuous. Your honeymoon may have been heavenly . . . or more down-to-earth. But in any case, you and your spouse-to-be were drawn to that moment of marriage by a dream—a dream of spending the rest of your days with the love of your life. Your heart was filled with hope, expectation, promise, and a dream that your marriage not only would be good, but would be a love that would last forever.

Since that day, your marriage has probably had its share of ups and downs. You've probably done or said some things that hurt your spouse—and vice versa. Perhaps you're still angry or bitter over harsh words, something done, or something *not* done.

Perhaps rekindling your love just doesn't seem to be possible.

But bringing back the dream is just what you need to have a great marriage.

The dream can live again, even stronger than ever. That's the purpose of this process you have embarked upon as a couple—to reawaken the dream and discover the love of your life all over again.

Prior to beginning this study, you were asked to read chapters 1–3 and complete the marriage map self-tests (also located in appendix B). If you have not already done so, you need to complete those questions. You can photocopy the pages from appendix B so that you and your spouse can fill out the charts separately. The marriage map includes seven stops on the marriage journey from that first dreamy love all the way to divorce. Marriages that end in divorce have traveled along the map, unable (or unwilling) to stop and turn around. Decide where you think you are on the marriage map, and then answer the questions below.

1. Look back over your marks, and write below which "stop" you believe you are at right now in your marriage. Then explain why.

   _____

   _____

   _____

2. Take a few moments to carefully consider the following statements. Circle the number on the lines (1 meaning "never"; 5 meaning "always") that describes how you feel in your marriage relationship.

   I feel accepted by and connected with my spouse.

   1   2   3   4   5

   I feel understood and honored by my spouse.

   1   2   3   4   5

   I feel bonded and rooted in this relationship.

   1   2   3   4   5

   I feel safe and secure in this relationship.

   1   2   3   4   5

   I feel cherished and deeply loved.

   1   2   3   4   5

   I feel that my spouse is committed and faithful.

   1   2   3   4   5

3. Which of these categories is most important to you?

   In my marriage, I need to feel _____

   _____

   _____

4. Why do you think such a feeling is so important to you in your marriage?

_____

_____

_____

5. Which of these categories would you guess is most important to your spouse?

    In our marriage, my spouse needs to feel _____

    _____

    _____

6. Why do you think such a feeling is so important to your spouse?

    _____

    _____

    _____

    Take a few moments to meditate on these categories, and ask God to impress
    upon your heart how your spouse would feel if the two of you were to be able to
    love each other in ways that would meet your deepest needs.

7. Conclude this Personal Reflection exercise by praying and writing a prayer that
    expresses the following:

    Lord, I thank you for my spouse, because _____

    _____

    I pray for my marriage and ask that you will _____

    _____

    I pray for my spouse and ask you to bless him/her by _____

    _____

    Please help me to better love my spouse. Show me what I can do to meet his/her needs.
    Amen.

Week One—Day Two

COUPLE INTERACTION:
LEARNING TO FORGIVE

Remember that during this week you need to read part 2—chapters 4 and 5 of *Divorce-Proof Your Marriage*. Then work together with your spouse to answer the following questions:

1. In Jeremiah 29:11, God told his people:

    "For I know the plans I have for you," says the Lord. "They are plans for good and not for disaster, to give you a future and a hope."

    Do you believe that God's plans for you—and your marriage—are "plans for good and not for disaster, to give you a future and a hope"?

    ❑ Yes   ❑ At this point, I'm not sure I really believe that.

2. Next, turn back to the Personal Reflection exercise you did on Day One. Each of you share where you think you are on the marriage map, and why.

    Turn to your spouse (husband, go first) and say something like,
    "I want to know what's important *to you* in our marriage."
    "I want to listen as you share your feelings."
    "I want to focus on hearing the desires of your heart for our marriage."

Then share the numbers you placed on the lines, as well as what you thought was the most important to both you and your spouse. Are these the same? Discuss your perceptions. Then on the line below, write what your spouse said was most important to him/her.

The category most important to my spouse was _____

3. Discuss how you currently handle it when one of you hurts the other (intention-
   ally or unintentionally). Could this eventually lead to danger for your marriage?
   How?

   _____

   _____

   _____

4. Is there unresolved conflict on which you need to "close the loop"? What steps
   do you both need to take in order to work toward that outcome?

   _____

   _____

   _____

   Gary and Barb say:
   Forgiving love disposes of the wrongs done against you—and done by you. It allows you to
   see your spouse as if he or she has done nothing wrong. Can you imagine picking up your
   relationship as if the behavior never happened? It's a divine makeover, a fresh chance to
   make the right choices. You are free to accept and connect with each other again.
   (from chapter 4, under heading "What Is Forgiving Love?")

Remembering that the Bible says, "Love each other with genuine affection, and take
delight in honoring each other" (Romans 12:10), take each other's hands, look each
other in the eyes, and share your desire to work toward a forgiving love that will
help you heal hurts and help you feel accept and connected with each other.

Conclude this Couple Interaction exercise by thanking God aloud for your spouse
and for his good plans for your marriage—filled with hope and a bright future.

Week One — Day Three

MY ASSIGNMENT:
LEARNING TO FORGIVE

You have two assignments this week:

1. Read part 2—chapters 4 and 5 of *Divorce-Proof Your Marriage*.
    Have you completed that assignment yet?

    ❑ Yes   ❑ No   ❑ I've started, but I have more to read.

2. Practice showing forgiving love to your spouse.

Your assignment is to unconditionally forgive your spouse this week for a minor offense. Try this approach: The next time your spouse does something that hurts you, take a brief moment in your heart to forgive him/her. Then, as soon as it is possible, walk up to your spouse, give him or her a hug, and say, "Do you know how much I love you?" Hug your spouse, and then walk away. There is no need to remind your spouse of what he or she has done. Just demonstrate God's forgiving love. For a more significant offense, the steps of closing the loop are found in chapter 3 of *Divorce-Proof Your Marriage*.

My Journal

How did your Couple Interaction time go? Were there any insights or breakthroughs? Explain.

_____

_____

_____

_____

_____

_____

_____

_____

_____

Here is what I did and how it went when I practiced forgiving love with my spouse.

_____

_____

_____

_____

_____

_____

_____

_____

_____

_____

Group Session Two

FORGIVE AND FORGET

SHARING AS A COUPLE

During the week, you and your spouse should have read part 2 of *Divorce-Proof Your Marriage*. Ideally you also made the time to work through the homework assignments so that you could discuss some aspects of forgiving love.

As this session begins, couples should work together to answer the following questions:

1. What are some reasons that you think people have a hard time forgiving their spouses? A few are listed; see if you can add more.

   ✓Pride
   Anger
   Discouragement
   Absence of love for spouse
   ✓ Poor communication
   Lack of compassion
   Hopelessness
   Holding a grudge
   Bitterness
   Fear of _____
   lack of desire
   family patterns
   not knowing how
   _____

2. From the list above, which of these obstacles might make it difficult for you to
    practice forgiving love? Write the obstacle, then a brief (less than a sentence)
    explanation of why this is a problem for you. One is given for you as an
    example.

    Pride – I think forgiveness makes me a weak person.
    I struggle most with (use as many spaces as needed):
    _____ because _____.
    _____ because _____.
    _____ because _____.

REDISCOVERING FORGIVING LOVE

Gary and Barb define forgiving love as follows:

Forgiving love heals hurts and helps spouses feel accepted and connected.

Forgiving love offers a fresh start after offenses both large and small. Forgiving love
safeguards your marriage by helping you feel accepted and connected. Forgiving love
is the first love every marriage needs in order to be divorce-proofed.

As a group, share some things you learned from reading the book or from your
homework assignments about forgiving love. Use the space below to write down
anything that strikes you, any new ideas you have received, or new insights from
others.

_____

_____

_____

The practice of forgiving love is not easy for everyone. At times it is very difficult to
forgive; at times it is very difficult to receive forgiveness.

Gary and Barb say,
Forgiveness—the ability to let go of past hurts—is perhaps the single most important
relationship skill we can develop in marriage. Keeping your spouse on the hook for past
offenses may give you a gratifying sense of power, but it always occurs at the expense of the
relationship. . . . No relationship can recover from serious disappointments and grow in
intimacy if one or both partners cannot let go of bitterness.
(from chapter 5, under heading "Granting Forgiveness")

Forgiveness sometimes gets a bad rap because some people have believed some myths about forgiveness that are just that—myths. These were discussed at length in chapters 4 and 5 of the book. See if you can fill in the blanks, then have your leader share the key words.

SOME MYTHS SURROUNDING FORGIVENESS:

Myth #1: "When I forgive, I must also ~~forget~~ ."
(The Bible never says we must forget the offenses.)

Myth #2: "The **hurt** is too great. It is **hard** for me to forgive."
(God would never command us to do something we cannot do.)

Myth #3: "I don't **feel** like forgiving, so my forgiveness can't be **genuine** ."
(Forgiveness is a choice, not a feeling.)

Myth #4: "I **can't** forgive unless the other person **ask** for it."
(We must forgive without conditions.)

Myth #5: "In order to forgive, I must **pretend** that **nothing** bad happened."
(If you have to forgive, then something happened. We are not to pretend.)

Myth #6: "I must forgive **immediately right away** or it **doesn't** **count** ."
(We are not to let anger fester, but we should be realistic.)

Chapter 5 in *Divorce-Proof Your Marriage* has pictures of the "Forgiveness "Loop." This "loop" describes a cycle of conflict. The "open loop" leaves conflict unaddressed and unresolved. Forgiveness closes the loop. When that happens, trust can be rebuilt and the relationship can be restored.

Gary and Barb say:

Every conflict with your spouse brings you to a fork in the road. After the offense has led to hurt and the hurt has turned to anger, you are faced with the choice of how to handle the situation … At first thought, it sure seems easier to ignore the problem, to shove aside the wrong you suffered—or the wrong you inflicted. But that quick fix won't last. It takes courage to restore and rebuild a relationship, regardless of which side of the offense you're on. It takes time, patience, trust, and maybe even some tears.
(from chapter 5, under heading "Where Are You in the Loop?")

3. Being able to forgive takes time. Gary and Barb suggest five biblical steps for sharing forgiving love and closing the loop on offense and hurt. As a group, fill in the blanks below as your leader offers the answers. After filling in the blanks for

each section, discuss as a group why this step is important in being able to close the loop and forgive.

STEP 1: PREPARE YOUR HEART   94-95

Read Philippians 2:3-5.

To prepare my heart, I need to __humble__ myself and __pray__. That way, I'll be more able to see my spouse's __perspective__. Then, I should look for the __underlying__ __cause__ of the conflict to truly understand what has __angered__ me. I will __commit__ to making my relationship with my spouse my __top__ __priority__.

In order to forgive, I need to prepare my heart because

_____

_____

_____

STEP 2: COMMUNICATE YOUR FEELINGS   97-98

Read James 1:19.

To communicate my feelings, I will __think__ __ahead__ about what I want to say so that I don't spout off with hurtful words. I will speak __kindly__ and __calmly__, and then I will __listen__. I will try to be __positive__, say what I mean, and not speak in __generalizations__. I will communicate __openly__ and __honestly__.

In order to forgive, I need to communicate my feelings because
__my spouse will not know what is going on. ~~I'll~~ never know__
__She'll__
__if I don't share__

_____

STEP 3: CONFRONT YOUR CONFLICTS

Read Ephesians 4:26-27.

My spouse and I are not __enimies__; we are on the same __team__. By working __together__, we can find a __solution__. To do this we will __choose__ an __appropriate__ __time__ and __setting__ to discuss our conflict. We will find out if we are __ready__ to discuss the issue. We will not assign __blame__. This kind of __loving__ __confrontation__ will help us close the loop.

In order to forgive, I need to confront the conflict because
__I don't want it to get worse__

_____

_____

STEP 4: FORGIVE YOUR SPOUSE

Read Mark 11:24-25.

Now the rubber meets the road. I not only must forgive, but I must __act__
out forgiveness. I may have to __request__ forgiveness, or I may have to
__grant__ forgiveness. The ability to __let__ __go__ of past hurts is perhaps the single most __important__ relationship __skill__ we can develop
in our marriage.

In order to forgive, I need to act out forgiveness because
__the bible says so. ~~brhme~~ Who am I not to forgive, when I have__
__been ~~every such~~ forgiven so much.__

STEP 5: REBUILD YOUR TRUST

Read 2 Corinthians 5:17-19.

__trust__ isn't rebuilt __overnight__. Yet through the power of
__Christ__ redeeming love, our marriage can be __transformed__ from
__rubble__ to __restoration__.

In order to forgive, I need to work to rebuild trust because
__I want to restore what was broken. I want my marriage to__
__be as God intended.__

4. Look back at the obstacle(s) you noted in question 2. On which of the five steps
above do you think you need to work in order to overcome that obstacle?
Why?

_____

_____

_____

**Remember that forgiving love heals hurts and helps
spouses feel accepted and connected.**

PREPARING FOR THE WEEK

*This week you will be looking more deeply at the topic of serving love. During the week, you
will need to read part 3—chapters 6 and 7 in Divorce-Proof Your Marriage. But don't
stop the forgiving love just because it's not on this week's assignment list! All of these loves
are vital to your marriage, and all will need to be practiced all the time. In fact, this week
you may need the forgiving love more than you did last week. Build on what you learn, communicate with each other, and above all, ask God to be with you. Ask for his guidance as
you seek to honor your spouse with serving love.*

Week Two—Day One

MY PERSONAL REFLECTION:
HOW CAN I SERVE YOU?

Remember that during this week you need to read part 3—chapters 6 and 7 of *Divorce-Proof Your Marriage*.

In a marriage, it isn't hard—and it doesn't take long—to move from the tingles of romance to the brass tacks of everyday life. Suddenly that man for whom you thought you would do anything is leaving his socks on the floor way too often. Suddenly that beautiful woman for whom you thought you would kiss the ground is nagging a bit too much about the socks on the floor.

The honeymoon is definitely over, and husbands and wives who love each other discover that the lack of feeling understood and honored begins to eat away at that love.

Cracks appear in our relationship with a spouse, and we don't know how to repair those cracks. Conflicts remain unresolved. Frustrations go unaddressed. Why? Because we've turned our focus back on ourselves and our needs. We don't want to serve, but we want to be served. We don't want to honor, but we want to be honored. So rather than healing, we experience a hardening of our hearts toward each other.

That's why it takes a serving love to make God's dreams for you come true. It takes a serving love to halt the slide of a marriage. It takes a serving love to begin to recognize your spouse's real needs and begin to serve him or her by meeting those needs. Spend a few moments and consider the following Scripture passages:

> Don't just pretend that you love others. Really love them. Hate what is wrong. Stand on the side of the good. Love each other with genuine affection, and take delight in honoring each other. (Romans 12:9-10)

After washing their feet, [Jesus] put on his robe again and sat down and asked, "Do you understand what I was doing? You call me 'Teacher' and 'Lord,' and you are right, because it is true. And since I, the Lord and Teacher, have washed your feet, you ought to wash each other's feet. I have given you an example to follow. Do as I have done to you. How true it is that a servant is not greater than the master. Nor are messengers more important than the one who sends them. You know these things—now do them! That is the path of blessing." (John 13:12-17)

1. Does your spouse need this kind of love? (circle one)

    (Yes)   No

2. Why does your spouse need this kind of love? (check any that apply)

    ☒ Because he/she needs to feel honored in this marriage.
    ☒ To fulfill God's dream for my marriage.
    ☒ Because I want to halt the slide of my marriage toward emotional divorce.
    ☒ Because my spouse deserves that kind of love.
    ☒ Because God loves me this way.
    ☒ Because it's the only way to begin the healing process.
    ☒ Because it will make our marriage better.

3. As you reflect on your attitudes toward your spouse, which of the characteristics below describe your current attitude toward your marriage? (Be honest!)

    ❏ Meet me half way.
    ❏ I should get what is rightfully mine.
    ☒ If you love me, I will love you back.
    ❏ When you contribute to this marriage, so will I.
    ❏ I love you just the way you are.
    ❏ I love you because Christ loves me.
    ❏ You do your part, and I'll do mine.

    ❏ I will serve you regardless of how you serve me.
    ❏ I love you in spite of what you do.
    ☒ I want to understand how to meet your needs.
    ☒ My feelings for you are not based on your feelings for me.
    ☒ I choose to forgive you.

4. Do any of the ones you checked convey an attitude that your love for your spouse is conditional?

(Yes)   No

If "yes," which ones? _If you love me, I will love you back_

5. Suggest actions you can take to demonstrate a serving love that will make your spouse feel honored and understood. Two examples are provided for you below.

❑ I will share with our children how much I appreciate everything my wife does for our family.
❑ I will schedule time to be alone with my husband and focus on his needs.

In order to demonstrate serving love to my spouse, I will…
Listen & so she feel understood. Be on the same team
so she knows she has a partner working towards the same
objective.

6. Take as much time as necessary now to pray, using the following pattern:

Thank God for your spouse.
Ask God to soften your heart toward your partner.
Ask for the humility to serve your spouse.
Ask God to show you how to identify your spouse's needs.
Ask God to keep those tender emotions close to the surface and to use them to impress on your spouse the sincerity of your love for him/her.

Week Two—Day Two

COUPLE INTERACTION:
HOW CAN I SERVE YOU?

Remember that during this week you need to read part 3—chapters 6 and 7 of *Divorce-Proof Your Marriage*. Then work together with your spouse to answer the following questions:

1. Read together Romans 12:9-10 and John 13:12-17. (These are quoted in the Day One lesson.)

2. Share with your spouse the attitudes that best describe you from question 3 in the Personal Reflection on Day One. Explain why you have these attitudes. As your spouse shares, identify his/her attitudes by writing your spouse's name next to them. (Husbands go first.)

3. Share your responses to question 5 in the Personal Reflection on Day One. (Wives go first.) Record below the actions your spouse intends to take to demonstrate a serving love for you.

    _____

    _____

    _____

4. Ask your spouse for three additional suggestions as to how you can serve him/her. Record below what your spouse would like you to do.
    My spouse would like me to serve him/her in the following ways:

    _____

    _____

Gary and Barb say,

When you become what your spouse needs, you are God's instrument of serving love. You complete your spouse. In the world's eyes, that's codependency; in God's eyes it is a true interdependence—a marriage of three: Jesus, husband, and wife. It is God's design. If you serve each other without meeting needs, your serving means little and leaves you both frustrated. But when you genuinely meet each other's needs out of the abundance of Christ's love in you, you become fulfilled persons.

(from chapter 6, under heading "The Benefits of Serving Love")

Conclude this Couple Interaction time in prayer by committing to serve your spouse in a way that will demonstrate honor. Place a check mark next to each of the three suggestions above as you commit to do these things for your spouse.

Week Two—Day Three

MY ASSIGNMENT:
HOW CAN I SERVE YOU?

You have two assignments this week:

1. Read part 3—chapters 6 and 7 of *Divorce-Proof Your Marriage.*
   Have you completed that assignment yet?

   ❏ Yes   ❏ No   ❏ I've started, but I have more to read.

2. Practice showing serving love to your spouse.
   Review the three suggestions your spouse gave you on how you can serve
   him/her. Give yourself a grade (on a scale of 1 to 5) for each of the three regarding how well you believe you did. The scale is below:

   1—Excellent; 2—Good; 3—Fair; 4—Poor; 5—Did not try.

   ❏ _____
   ❏ _____
   ❏ _____

My Journal

How did your Couple Interaction time go? Were there any insights or breakthroughs?
Explain.

_____
_____
_____

_____

_____

_____

_____

_____

_____

_____

Here is what I did and how it went when I practiced serving love.

_____

_____

_____

_____

_____

_____

_____

_____

_____

Group Session Three

THE PLACE OF SERVICE

SHARING AS A COUPLE

During the week, you and your spouse should have read part 3 of *Divorce-Proof Your Marriage*. Ideally you also made the time to work through the homework assignments so that you could discuss some aspects of serving love and then begin to put them into practice!

As this session begins, couples should work together to answer the following questions:

1. Consider the places you go where you receive "service," such as a restaurant, an auto repair shop, the dry cleaners, the grocery store check-out line. What defines "good service" in these areas? What are some of your pet peeves regarding bad service?

    taking advantage of people, not listening

    _____

    _____

Read John 13:1-5, and answer the following questions:

> Before the Passover celebration, Jesus knew that his hour had come to leave this world and return to his Father. He now showed the disciples the full extent of his love. It was time for supper, and the Devil had already enticed Judas, son of Simon Iscariot, to carry out his plan to betray Jesus. Jesus

knew that the Father had given him authority over everything and that he
had come from God and would return to God. So he got up from the table,
took off his robe, wrapped a towel around his waist, and poured water into
a basin. Then he began to wash the disciples' feet and to wipe them with
the towel he had around him.

2. Jesus met his disciples' needs by serving them. While his act of washing their feet
    symbolized his forgiveness of their sins, his act also demonstrated the heart of a
    servant. How can spouses have servants' hearts toward one another?

    By seeking out what other peoples needs
    are. Be the first to serve. Don't exept to
    be served back.

3. Why is this attitude so important in marriage?

    It shows unconditional love

We honor our spouse by serving him or her. As always, Jesus is our example.

REDISCOVERING SERVING LOVE

Gary and Barb define serving love as follows:

**Serving love discovers and meets needs and helps
spouses feel honored and understood.**

As a group, share some things you learned from reading the book or from your
homework assignments about serving love. Use the space below to write down
anything that strikes you, any new ideas you have received, or new insights from
others.

Read Romans 12:10, and then answer the following questions:

> Love each other with genuine affection, and take delight in honoring each other.

4. What does it mean to honor someone? As a group, share your ideas and record them below.

Honoring someone means that I respect them and value them. Make them comfortable. Give praise to them. Make them feel respected.

Gary and Barb say:

Serving love allows you both to feel honored and understood. If you want to feel understood, if you want to feel satisfied, if you want to feel honored, then build a marriage overflowing with serving love. If each of you is committed 100 percent to understanding and meeting the other's needs, then both of you will enjoy 100 percent honor and 100 percent understanding that result from that mutual commitment.
(from chapter 6, under heading "The Benefits of Serving Love")

5. Gary and Barb explain that marriage is not a 50/50 concept; instead, it should be a 100/100—that is, each spouse gives 100 percent to the marriage. How would you describe a 100/100 marriage? Why is the 100/100 concept vital for a healthy marriage?

Serve to serve, not to be served back.

Read Philippians 2:1-5:

> Is there any encouragement from belonging to Christ? Any comfort from his love? Any fellowship together in the Spirit? Are your hearts tender and sympathetic? Then make me truly happy by agreeing wholeheartedly with each other, loving one another, and working together with one heart and purpose. Don't be selfish; don't live to make a good impression on others. Be humble, thinking of others as better than yourself. Don't think only about your own affairs, but be interested in others, too, and what they are doing. Your attitude should be the same that Christ Jesus had.

6. Clearly God expects his people to be servants to one another—so our spouses are definitely included! How can spouses apply the above characteristics in their marriages? Give some examples.

Not seeking reward

_____

_____

_____

Practicing humility

_____

_____

_____

Practicing unselfishness

_____

_____

_____

Showing concern for the other

_____

_____

_____

Not demanding of personal rights and needs

_____

_____

_____

Knowing the needs

Ask, Remember when told. Focus on them

_____

_____

Sometimes the most difficult task a servant has is to know what the other person's needs are.

Gary and Barb say,

Barb and I believe that communication is indispensable to the ministry of serving love in marriage. Let's face it: None of us is a mind reader. If Barb doesn't communicate her needs to me, my chances of meeting those needs are mighty slim. And if I don't communicate my needs to her, she's flying blind when it comes to serving me. In a marriage relationship, discovering and meeting needs in an atmosphere of serving love presupposes that husband and wife are willing to talk. It is in the process of communication that needs are shared or discovered.

(from chapter 7, under heading "Communication: Key to Discovering and Meeting Needs")

7. Fill in the following charts:

   On a scale of 1 to 5 (1 is "I don't know anything"; 5 is "I know everything and am a mind reader"), plot how well you think you do at knowing your spouse's needs.

   1   2   3   ()   4   5

   Now plot how well you think you do at expressing your needs to your spouse. (1 is "I think he/she should know without my saying anything"; 5 is "I spout out my needs all the time, so there's no room for doubt").

   1   2   3   4   5

8. Why is communication of needs vital in order for spouses to be able to act in serving love toward one another?

   _____

   _____

9. Review the five levels of communication in the book. Your leader will help you fill in the blanks. Then give some examples of this kind of communication.

SHARING GENERAL INFORMATION

   We speak largely in _____.

   An example of sharing general information:

   _____

   _____

SHARING FACTS

We discuss ___people___ and ___events___, but nothing ___personal___.
An example of sharing facts:

_____

_____

_____

SHARING OPINIONS AND BELIEFS

We share ___personal___ ___information___, but nothing too ___risky___.
An example of sharing opinions and beliefs:

_____

_____

_____

SHARING FEELINGS AND EMOTIONS

We begin to ___open___ our ___hearts___.
An example of sharing feelings and emotions:

_____

_____

_____

SHARING NEEDS, INTIMATE CONCERNS, HOPES, AND FEARS

We ___volunerable___ share our ___heart___ of hearts.
An example of needs and concerns, hopes and fears:

_____

_____

**Remember that serving love discovers and meets needs
and helps spouses feel honored and understood.**

PREPARING FOR THE WEEK

This week you will be looking more deeply at the topic of persevering love. You will need to read part 4—chapters 8 and 9 of Divorce-Proof Your Marriage. *Consider how you and your spouse can focus on the quality of persevering love that will help you weather any difficulties you're facing.*

Week Three—Day One

MY PERSONAL REFLECTION:
SURVIVING THE STORMS OF LIFE

How would persevering love affect your marriage? Consider the verse you looked at during the group session from the famous "love chapter," 1 Corinthians 13.

> Love never gives up, never loses faith, is always hopeful, and endures through every circumstance. (1 Corinthians 13:7)

Can you imagine why such love is crucial to fulfilling God's dreams for your marriage? Without persevering love like that, the storms and stresses of life will tend to beat against a marriage and erode it, until it finally falls apart. But persevering love endures through every circumstance. Take a few moments to consider the effect of this kind of love on you and your spouse by meditating on what it would be like to know and feel that kind of love from your spouse. Complete the following sentences as thoughtfully and as thoroughly as possible:

1. Knowing that my spouse loves me with a love that never gives up would make me feel:

   _____

   _____

   _____

2. Knowing that my spouse loves me with a love that never loses faith in our marriage would make me feel:

   _____

_____

_____

3. Knowing that my spouse loves me with a love that is always hopeful would make me feel:

_____

_____

_____

4. Knowing that my spouse loves me with a love that endures through every circumstance would make me feel:

_____

_____

_____

5. Is persevering love present in your marriage now? Which of the above has been most present in your relationship? Check one.

❑ A love that never gives up
❑ A love that never loses faith
❑ A love that is always hopeful
❑ A love that endures through every circumstance

6. Consider a present or past trial that affected your marriage. What can/did you do to grow closer to your spouse through this trial? List your thoughts below.

_____

_____

_____

Take a few moments to meditate on the value of a persevering love, and ask God to impress upon your heart how it would bless your marriage if the two of you were to commit to learning more about developing persevering love in your marriage.

Week Three—Day Two

COUPLE INTERACTION:
SURVIVING THE STORMS OF LIFE

Remember that during this week you need to read part 4—chapters 8 and 9 of *Divorce-Proof Your Marriage*. Then work together with your spouse to answer the following questions:

Read together 1 Corinthians 13:7 (it is quoted on Day One).
Share from your Personal Reflection how you would feel if your spouse loved you with this persevering love. As your spouse shares, record his/her feelings below.

1. A love that never gives up would make my spouse feel:

   _____

   _____

   _____

2. A love that never loses faith in our marriage would make my spouse feel:

   _____

   _____

   _____

3. A love that is always hopeful would make my spouse feel:

   _____

   _____

4. A love that endures through every circumstance would make my spouse feel:

_____

_____

_____

5. Evaluate the presence of persevering love in your marriage now. Share your responses to question 5 on Day One. Note how your spouse responded to the question of which of these has been most present in your relationship.

❑ A love that never gives up
❑ A love that never loses faith
❑ A love that is always hopeful
❑ A love that endures through every circumstance

6. Is one of these characteristics noticeably absent? If so, which one? Discuss what you need to do to help make that characteristic of persevering love a reality in your marriage.

Conclude your time together by asking God to help each of you follow through on your commitment to love each other with a persevering love.

Week Three—Day Three

MY ASSIGNMENT:
SURVIVING THE STORMS OF LIFE

You have two assignments this week:

1. Read part 4—chapters 8 and 9 of *Divorce-Proof Your Marriage*.
    Have you completed that assignment yet?

    ❑ Yes   ❑ No   ❑ I've started, but I have more to read.

2. Practice showing persevering love to your spouse.

Review the characteristics of persevering love that are present in your marriage, as
well as those that you think could be improved upon. Grade yourself with the old-
fashioned A to F that you used to get on report cards by answering the following
statements:

    I don't give up when difficulties hit our marriage. _____
    I don't lose faith in God's dream for our marriage. _____
    I am hopeful of what God will do in us and through us. _____
    I am able to endure through even the most difficult circumstances. _____

My Journal

How did your Couple Interaction time go? Were there any insights or breakthroughs?
Explain.

_____

_____

_____

_____

_____

_____

_____

_____

_____

_____

Here is what I did and how it went when I practiced persevering love.

_____

_____

_____

_____

_____

_____

_____

_____

_____

_____

Group Session Four

GROW THROUGH TRIALS

SHARING AS A COUPLE

During the week, you and your spouse should have read part 4 of *Divorce-Proof Your Marriage*. Ideally you also made the time to work through the homework assignments so that you could discuss some aspects of persevering love and then begin to put them into practice!

As this session begins, couples should work together to answer the following questions:

1. What are some kinds of trials marriages can face? Suggest the types of trials that can put pressure on a marriage. Two are provided as examples.

    Loss of a job
    Conflict with extended family
    divorse in the family
    differences in parenting styles.
    infadelities
    different life styles.
    addictions
    different personalities
    change of jobs
    health of children

2. Describe some ways that you've seen other married couples deal with these kinds of conflicts.

ignore them, run away. (Neg). Communication, counseling sharing feelings (Pos)

Read 1 Corinthians 13:7.

> Love <u>never</u> gives up, never loses faith, is always hopeful, and <u>endures</u> through every circumstance.

3. What do you think would happen in many marriages if the spouses adopted this definition for their love?

Never loose hope, weather any storm.

REDISCOVERING PERSEVERING LOVE

Gary and Barb define persevering love as follows:

Persevering love stays strong in tough times and helps spouses feel bonded—best friends for life.

Spend a few minutes sharing why it is so important for spouses to be able to <u>depend</u> on each other's persevering love. Write below any insights you receive about how persevering love has helped other couples.

Gary and Barb say,
The unconditional acceptance of persevering love says, "No matter how good or bad you look, no matter how much money you earn or lose, no matter how smart or feebleminded you are, I will still love you." That's the stuff of our wedding vows—for better or for worse, for richer or for poorer, in sickness and in health. Persevering love chooses to continue loving even when life dumps on us a world of reasons to fall out of love.
(from chapter 8, under heading "Persevering Love Requires Unconditional Acceptance")

4. What does God's persevering love look like? After each verse below, write the characteristics of God's persevering love:

> Understand, therefore, that the Lord your God is indeed God. He is the faithful God who keeps his covenant for a thousand generations and constantly loves those who love him and obey his commands. (Deuteronomy 7:9)

Alway constant, Faithful, Keeps His promises, enduring.

> How precious is your unfailing love, O God! All humanity finds shelter in the shadow of your wings. (Psalm 36:7)

love is unfailing, ~~close~~ you need to be close to him

> "For the mountains may depart and the hills disappear, but even then I will remain loyal to you. My covenant of blessing will never be broken," says the Lord, who has mercy on you. (Isaiah 54:10)

loyal, un deserved, unbreakable, enduring

> "I command you to love each other in the same way that I love you. And here is how to measure it—the greatest love is shown when people lay down their lives for their friends." (John 15:12-13)

unselfish, willing to give everything.

Clearly God loves us with persevering love. Think about it—we disappoint him every day. We often ignore him. Sometimes we outright deny him. All that, and yet he still loves us. He promises to stay with us.

Gary and Barb say,

In your times of crisis and unbearable stress, you may secretly wonder if your spouse will draw closer to you and stand with you, no matter what, or turn away and let you battle the storm alone. You may also wonder if you have the strength to hang in there with your spouse or if you will be tempted to walk away. Now is the time to decide and agree together: Together we will tackle anything that comes our way, and we will stay together in it no matter where it goes.

(from chapter 9, under heading "Decide to Tackle Trouble Together—Wherever It Takes You")

5. Gary and Barb discuss "bricks" for building a love that perseveres. As the leader gives you the answers to the blanks below, write in the words. Then answer the questions.

BRICK #1: CONNECT AND STAY CONNECTED

Your ability to __ability__ together in the hard times is directly __endure__ to the __depth__ of your __partenership__ in good times. To stay glued together in __difizulties__, you have to apply the cement of partnership in the __good__ times.

What can spouses do to connect with each other during the good times? As a group, list some ideas below.

❏ Before you get out of bed every morning, tell your spouse that you love him/her.

❏ _every day make live easier for them._

❏ _____

❏ _____

❏ _____

BRICK #2: MAKE YOUR RELATIONSHIP A SAFE PLACE

You spouse needs to know that your __loving__ __arms__ will always be a __shelter__ in the midst of a __trial__ or __tradegy__.

When might spouses need a "safe place" in their marriage?

when they're hurt, insufficient ,

_____

_____

BRICK #3: KEEP COMMUNICATING

Trials can drive a ___wedge___ between a husband and wife. It is important to communicate and be the best ___help___ you can be.

In what ways do trials drive a wedge between spouses?

disagreeing with trial, different personalities.
(how to handle the)

BRICK #4: REST IN THE TRUTH THAT GOD HAS A PURPOSE FOR TRIALS

Great marriages are often forged through ___difficult___ ___trials___.
Acknowledge that God has a ___purpose___ in the trials to build your
___character___.

How can spouses hang on to the truth of God's purpose in their trial?

Keep sight of what God is doing is your life.

BRICK #5: DECIDE TO TACKLE TROUBLE TOGETHER—WHEREVER IT TAKES YOU

When you commit to this level of ___persevering love___, you are offering
your spouse the ___assurance___ that he or she will never be ___alone___ when
___trials___ come.

**Remember that persevering love stays <u>strong</u> in <u>tough</u>
<u>times</u> and helps spouses feel bonded—best friends for life.**

PREPARING FOR THE WEEK

This week you will be looking more deeply at the topic of guarding love. You will need to read part 5—chapters 10 and 11 of Divorce-Proof Your Marriage. *Consider how you can continue to build up the bricks that will help your marriage to persevere no matter what.*

Week Four—Day One

MY PERSONAL REFLECTION:
GUARDING YOUR HEART

You might find it hard to believe that your heart could ever drift from your husband or wife. Or you may not be able to imagine that your heart, which was meant to be given to your spouse alone, could ever become poisoned by other loves. But the Bible warns us all:

> If you think you are standing strong, be careful, for you, too, may fall into the same sin. (1 Corinthians 10:12)

1. Reflect on the following statements to help you assess if your heart may be currently influenced by threats to your marriage:

I am currently hiding sin in my heart that would damage our marriage if my spouse knew about it.
❑ Yes ☑ No ❑ Not sure

I feel that my job/career keeps me from spending enough time with my spouse.
❑ Yes ☑ No ❑ Not sure

I feel that my spouse has other interests that are more important than me.
❑ Yes ❑ No ❑ Not sure ☑ Sometimes

I feel that my love for my spouse is not what it once was.
❑ Yes ☑ No ❑ Not sure

If you answered "yes" to any of these statements, then you realize that your heart is being threatened by enemies seeking to destroy your marriage. If so, you have several options:

❏ You can confide in a close and trusted Christian friend to help you fight this enemy.
❏ You can share your struggle with your spouse and fight this threat together.
❏ You can decide today to adopt God's guarding love and defeat this threat. It is *never too late* to start guarding your heart.
❏ You can spend more time in prayer and the study of God's Word to gain confidence that God will fight for you. Your heart needs to be encouraged that his love is more powerful than any threat to your marriage.
❏ You can decide not to give up. God's love can provide a way to defeat the threat and he can give your marriage a fresh, new start!

2. Communicate your resolve to practice guarding love. This exercise will help you communicate to your spouse that you will guard your heart and that together the two of you will guard your marriage. Provided below is a pattern that is found in Psalm 121:1-8. The left-hand column contains the testimony of God's guarding love for you. The column on the right contains space for you to compose your own declaration to your spouse.

God's Promise

I look up to the mountains—
    does my help come from there?

My help comes from the Lord,
    who made the heavens and the
        earth!

He will not let you stumble and fall;
    the one who watches over you will
        not sleep.

Indeed, he who watches over Israel
    never tires and never sleeps.

My Promise

I'll guard my wife's heart

I'll pray with her

God's Promise   **My Promise**

The Lord himself watches over you!
    The Lord stands beside you as your
        protective shade.

The sun will not hurt you by day,
    nor the moon at night.   I'll protect my wife

The Lord keeps you from all evil
    and preserves your life

The Lord keeps watch over you as you   i'll be a leader my wife
        come and go,   can follow
    both now and forever.

Week Four—Day Two

COUPLE INTERACTION:
GUARDING YOUR HEART

Remember that during this week you need to read part 5—chapters 10 and 11 of *Divorce-Proof Your Marriage*. Then share with your spouse the declarations you prepared in Day One. On the chart below, write what your spouse declared to you in the space provided:

God's Promise

I look up to the mountains—
 does my help come from there?

My help comes from the Lord,
 who made the heavens and the earth!

He will not let you stumble and fall;
 the one who watches over you will
  not sleep.

Indeed, he who watches over Israel
 never tires and never sleeps.

The Lord himself watches over you!
 The Lord stands beside you as your
  protective shade.

My Spouse's Promise

I'll seek God for help with my own faults and for our marriage.

I will help you when you'll stumble and lift you up when you fall.

I will stand besides you always.

I will stay away from evil and cling to what is good

God's Promise   **My Spouse's Promise**

The sun will not hurt you by day,
    nor the moon at night.

The Lord keeps you from all evil
    and preserves your life

The Lord keeps watch over you as you
       come and go,
    both now and forever.

Week Four—Day Three

MY ASSIGNMENT:
GUARDING YOUR HEART

You have two assignments this week:

1. Read part 5—chapters 10 and 11 of *Divorce-Proof Your Marriage*. Have you completed that assignment yet?

   ☑ Yes   ☐ No   ☐ I've started, but I have more to read.

2. Practice showing guarding love to your spouse. Cut out a picture of a castle from a magazine or newspaper and put it in a place where you will always see it (your computer at work, in your wallet, on the dashboard, on your refrigerator). Use this as a constant reminder to guard your marriage castle.

My Journal

How did your Couple Interaction time go? Were there any insights or breakthroughs? Explain.

____quickly_____

_____

_____

_____

_____

_____

_____

not consistant

_____

_____

Here is what I did and how it went when I practiced guarding love.

_____

_____

_____

_____

_____

_____

_____

_____

_____

Group Session Five

DEFEAT THE ENEMIES AT THE GATE

SHARING AS A COUPLE

During the week, you and your spouse should have read part 5 of *Divorce-Proof Your Marriage*. Ideally you also made the time to work through the homework assignments so that you could discuss some aspects of guarding love and then begin to put them into practice!

As this session begins, couples should work together to answer the following questions:

1. Describe what these different "guards" do for you:
   Security guard _protects and guard_
   Lifeguard _Saves your life_
   Guard rail _Support from faily, keeps you own your path_
   Mouth guard _protect you from saying the wrong thing_
   Guard dog _alway watching over you._

2. God wants us to have a "heart guard" as well. Read the following verse:

   Above all else, guard your heart, for it affects everything you do.
   (Proverbs 4:23)

   What do you think a "heart guard" should do? _protect your life and heart_

3. Talk about the importance of seeing your marriage as a castle, a fortress. Talk about being realistic about the fiery arrows that Satan would like to launch at you. How can you begin to protect your marriage?

aviod the obvious, pray daily.

REDISCOVERING GUARDING LOVE

Gary and Barb define guarding love as follows:

Guarding love protects from threats and helps spouses feel safe and secure.

Spend a few minutes sharing why it is so important for spouses to view their marriages as castles and to guard them diligently. Write below any insights you receive about how guarding love has helped other couples:

God instructs us to. My marriage is a target and society w/ devil wants to bring in down, this is a reason to protect it.

Perhaps you feel "Nothing will ever tempt me away from my spouse. I'm as pure as the wind-driven snow." Well, the Bible has a couple of words for you . . .

> Pride goes before destruction, and haughtiness before a fall. (Proverbs 16:18)

> If you think you are standing strong, be careful, for you, too, may fall into the same sin. (1 Corinthians 10:12)

God knows us so well! He knows how weak we are. That's precisely why we need guarding love—not pride, not a "better than others" attitude—but a commitment to guarding love.

4. As your leader reads, fill in the blanks that further describe guarding love. The instruction to "guard your heart" means to _purposely_ place a _protective_ _shield_ around the center of your life. You need to post a _watch_ and exercise great _care_. When you guard your heart, you

are guarding all that is truly __valuable__ in life. It will protect your marriage from both __internal__ and __external__ threats.

Gary and Barb say,

Guarding love will serve your marriage the way ancient castles served their inhabitants. Guarding love will help you fend off attacks on your marriage from without and within. Guarding love will keep your focus where it belongs—fixed on your first love. Without guarding love, you risk disconnecting from each other and connecting to other people, things, or activities that will pull you away from your spouse.
(from chapter 10, under heading "Are You Prepared for the Battle?")

Let's consider what the husband and wife need to do in order to guard their hearts and protect their marriages. Gary and Barb discuss key ways that a husband can guard his wife's heart and ways that a wife can guard her husband's heart. Split into two groups—men in one group and women in another. Then discuss the questions in the appropriate section below.

FOR THE WOMEN:
These questions are based on chapter 11, "Building Walls of Protection" under the heading "Seven Keys to Guarding Your Husband's Heart" in *Divorce-Proof Your Marriage*. Refer to the book if needed.

What are some ways you can honor your husband and his world? How can you continue to dream big dreams with him?

_____
_____
_____

Have you ever sabotaged your husband by wounding him in some way? What happened? How did you make it right?

_____
_____
_____

Why is unconditional love so important in a marriage?

_____
_____
_____

In what ways do/should you understand your husband's "maleness" and work within that framework?

_____

_____

_____

In what ways do/can you encourage his male friendships?

_____

_____

_____

In what ways do you see yourself completing your husband? How would you describe the teamwork in your marriage?

_____

_____

_____

Do you commit yourself to your husband and to God? How does he know that?

_____

_____

_____

FOR THE MEN:

These questions are based on chapter 11, "Building Walls of Protection" under the heading "Seven Keys to Guarding Your Wife's Heart" in *Divorce-Proof Your Marriage*. Refer to the book if needed.

Do you truly listen to your wife or do you always jump in with your logical answers to her problems? What can you do better?

_____ Ask what you can do to help _____

_____

What kind of practical help could your wife use on a day-to-day basis?

_____ ask her for something specific _____

_____

Why is it important that you make time to be alone with your wife? What are you going to do to make that happen in the next couple weeks?

_____

_____

_____

Why is it important that you give your wife some time for herself? What are you going to do to make that happen in the next couple weeks?

_____

_____

_____

Why is unconditional love so important in a marriage?

_____

_____

_____

In what ways do you demonstrate spiritual leadership in your home?

_____

_____

_____

Do you pray for and with your wife? How has that helped your marriage?

_____

_____

_____

Gary and Barb say,

Gary and I want to strongly admonish you to continually pursue guarding love for your relationship. We need to be vigilant in guarding the love of our lives. Any of the external and internal threats we have mentioned can pollute an unguarded heart and poison your marriage. No matter how positive your legacy as a couple may be at this point, the enemy will continue to pound at your gate, attempting to steal your dream and nullify your example to others. He knows that in one single unguarded moment you can lose your testimony, your platform for counsel, and your positive influence.

(from chapter 10, under heading "Treasures Worth Guarding")

**Remember that guarding love protects from threats and
helps spouses feel safe and secure.**

PREPARING FOR THE WEEK

*This week you will be looking more deeply at the topic of celebrating love. You will need to
read part 6—chapters 12 and 13 of* Divorce-Proof Your Marriage. *When you get
home, put one of your wedding pictures front and center where you both will see it every
day. Remind yourselves to* celebrate!

Week Five—Day One

MY PERSONAL REFLECTION:
LET'S CELEBRATE!

Everyone likes a celebration! And can you imagine how great it would have felt in high school to have been given a homework assignment to "go celebrate"? Well, you're in luck. Your assignment this week, should you choose to accept it, is to celebrate your marriage.

How will you communicate a celebrating love? Fill in the blanks below to help you begin to think about all the things you can celebrate about your spouse.

1. Ten things I love about my spouse:

   _____
   _____
   _____
   _____
   _____
   _____
   _____
   _____
   _____
   _____

2. Select from the list below statements that genuinely reflect your feelings.

   ❑ I'd like to experience what it's like to have you celebrate me and enjoy being with me.
   ❑ I'd love to feel what it's like to know you've been thinking about me all day.

❏ I want to laugh with you more often.

❏ I want to rekindle the romance in our relationship.

❏ I want to learn again how to date you.

❏ I'm willing to learn again how to give you my undivided attention.

❏ I long to more often experience your undivided attention.

❏ If I felt your undivided attention from time to time, it would make me feel . . .

❏ I want to feel that head-over-heels-in-love feeling with you again.

❏ I want you to fall head-over-heels in love with me again.

❏ If I knew you were head-over-heels in love with me again, it would make me feel . . .

❏ I want us to feel close again, as close as we felt when . . .

❏ If I knew you were committed to loving me with a celebrating love, it would make me feel . . .

Read Proverbs 5:18-20 and Song of Songs 7:1—8:7.

Pray for God's guidance as you seek to celebrate your spouse this week.

Week Five—Day Two

COUPLE INTERACTION:
LET'S CELEBRATE!

Remember that during this week you need to read part 6—chapters 12 and 13 of *Divorce-Proof Your Marriage*.

Turn to your spouse (husband, go first), and share your answers to the questions for Day One. Share the true feelings of your heart about what you desire for your marriage. Take your time, and make this exercise a time to celebrate your deepest desires for your spouse and your marriage. Ask your spouse to suggest other things he/she would like to hear you say.

1. Ten things my spouse loves about me:

    _____

    _____

    _____

    _____

    _____

    _____

    _____

    _____

    _____

    _____

2. Check below the statements your spouse checked from Day One.

   Statement my husband/wife checked:
   ❏ I'd like to experience what it's like to have you celebrate me and enjoy being with me.
   ❏ I'd love to feel what it's like to know you've been thinking about me all day.
   ❏ I want to laugh with you more often.
   ❏ I want to rekindle the romance in our relationship.
   ❏ I want to learn again how to date you.
   ❏ I'm willing to learn again how to give you my undivided attention.
   ❏ I long to more often experience your undivided attention.
   ❏ If I felt your undivided attention from time to time, it would make me feel . . .
   ❏ I want to feel that head-over-heels-in-love feeling with you again.
   ❏ I want you to fall head-over-heels in love with me again.
   ❏ If I knew you were head-over-heels in love with me again, it would make me feel . . .
   ❏ I want us to feel close again, as close as we felt when . . .
   ❏ If I knew you were committed to loving me with a celebrating love, it would make me feel . . .

3. Can you commit together to making a celebrating love a permanent "fixture" in your marriage? Are you willing to put forth as much effort as necessary to make your spouse experience the joy of having you take great delight and rejoice over him/her? If so, read the following prayer of commitment as indicated:

   Husband: God, I thank you that you love my wife with a celebrating love.
   Wife: I thank you that you love my husband with a celebrating love.

   Husband: Help her to sense your great delight in her.
   Wife: Help him to feel you rejoicing over him.
   Both: Quiet us both with your love, and help our marriage to reflect more of your love.

   Husband: Help me to learn more and more about how to touch her heart with a celebrating love.
   Wife: Help me to learn more and more about how to bless him with a celebrating love.

   Husband: Lord, I commit to the process of learning ways to love her with a celebrating love.
   Wife: I commit to the process of learning ways to love him with a celebrating love.
   Both: Help us to recapture the romance, recover the joy, and make our marriage a party that brings joy to us and to you. In Jesus' name, Amen.

Week Five—Day Three

MY ASSIGNMENT:
LET'S CELEBRATE!

You have two assignments this week:

1. Read part 6—chapters 12 and 13 of *Divorce-Proof Your Marriage*.
    Have you completed that assignment yet?

    ❏ Yes   ❏ No   ❏ I've started, but I have more to read.

2. Go out on a date and celebrate your marriage!

My Journal

How did your Couple Interaction time go? Were there any insights or breakthroughs?
Explain.

_____

_____

_____

_____

_____

_____

_____

_____

_____

_____

Here is what I did and how it went when I practiced celebrating love.

_____

_____

_____

_____

_____

_____

_____

_____

_____

_____

Group Session Six

CELEBRATE WHAT GOD HAS GIVEN

SHARING AS A COUPLE

During the week, you and your spouse should have read part 6 of *Divorce-Proof Your Marriage.* Ideally you also made the time to work through the homework assignments so that you could discuss some aspects of celebrating love and then begin to put them into practice!

As this session begins, couples should work together to answer the following questions:

1. Write a paragraph about your wedding day. Try to remember how you felt when you made your vows to each other.

   _____

   _____

   _____

   _____

2. What things happen in marriages to take the glorious celebration out of them?

   _____

   _____

   _____

   _____

   _____

REDISCOVERING CELEBRATING LOVE

Marriages need celebrating love in order to stay strong. Gary and Barb define celebrating love as follows:

Celebrating love rejoices in the marriage relationship and helps spouses feel cherished and captivated.

Spend a few minutes sharing some of the ideas people used to celebrate during the past week. Write below any insights you receive about how celebrating love has helped other couples:

_____

_____

_____

_____

_____

Celebrations don't happen naturally. Your wedding did not just occur; we can bet that months of planning went into that memorable celebration. When you want to have a birthday party or a retirement party or any other kind of celebration, you need to plan ahead. Well, the same is true for celebrating your marriage. It takes a little bit of work. You'll need to *think* about it, plan for it, and act on it even when you don't feel like it. But we can promise you this: it will be worth it!

3. As your leader reads, fill in the blanks that further describe celebrating love.

PUT EACH OTHER AT THE TOP OF THE LIST

The first key to celebrating love is to move each other to the ___top___ of your ~~to-do~~ list. You need __quality__ time. Find __enjoyable__ __activities__ to do together. Don't give each other __leftover__ time.

CONFESS TO EACH OTHER

__unresolved__ __conflict__ block all kinds of intimacy. Close the __forgiveness__ __loop__ when you sense a __wall__ between you and your spouse.

GET TO KNOW EACH OTHER AGAIN

Demonstrate your __love__ by showing that you are __deeply__ __interested__ in your spouse. Rediscover each other's __strengths__, __personal__ __interest__, and __uniqueness__.

RETHINK YOUR THINKING

Ask God to __refresh__ your __love__ for your spouse. Be willing to __fall__ __in__ __love__ with your spouse all over again.

REKINDLE ROMANCE AND PHYSICAL INTIMACY

Both spouses need to understand the different __intimacy__ needs they have. Women need to __talk__ and have __emotional,__ __intimacy__; for men, intimacy is found in the __sexual__ __relationship__.

4. Using the keys above for guidance, share as many ways as you can think of to celebrate your love for your spouse. Use the lines below to record everyone's thoughts.

   __laugh together__

   _____

   _____

   _____

Celebrating love is vitally important. Gary and Barb make the point that a key to this kind of love is a "God-thing"—in other words, it is the spiritual relationship that binds husband and wife together with a third party—Christ himself.

Read Ecclesiastes 4:12.

> A person standing alone can be attacked and defeated, but two can stand back-to-back and conquer. Three are even better, for a triple-braided cord is not easily broken.

5. Why is spiritual intimacy a vital part of a Christian marriage?

   _____

   _____

   _____

6. How can spiritual intimacy help you . . . have the grace to show forgiving love?

   _____

   _____

   _____

have the humility to show serving love?

_____

_____

_____

have the patience to show persevering love?

_____

_____

_____

have the wisdom to show guarding love?

_____

_____

_____

have the joy to show celebrating love?

_____

_____

_____

have the power to show renewing love?

_____

_____

_____

7. What kinds of activities / attitudes would characterize a couple with strong spiritual intimacy?

_____

_____

_____

8. What kinds of activities / attitudes could be roadblocks to a couple's spiritual intimacy?

_____

_____

9. How can the husband and the wife encourage each other to personal spiritual growth?

_____

_____

_____

Gary and Barb say,
Celebrating love revels in the emotional, physical, and spiritual connections that bond you to your spouse. It's a love that protects you and your spouse from drifting apart and enables you to fall in love and feel discovered all over again. Celebrating love rejoices daily in the marriage you have and helps you feel cherished and captivated by each other. Celebration is an inescapable element of God's love.
(from chapter 12, under heading "Love Worth Celebrating")

Remember that celebrating love rejoices in the marriage relationship and helps spouses feel cherished and captivated.

PREPARING FOR THE WEEK

This week you will be looking more deeply at the topic of renewing love. You will need to read part 7—chapters 14 and 15 of Divorce-Proof Your Marriage. *Be sure to complete the three days of assignments.*

Kathy - surgery Tuesday
Warners - doing much better - everything falling into place
Dochtermans - leaving Wed. for Yosemite → Sunday
Barnes - Karen taking depression meds. and starting counseling
Oronoz - Celeste still sick - bronchitis and sinus infection
Edwards - Dave graduates May 28th - show in mid-April

MY PERSONAL REFLECTION:
RENEWING THE COMMITMENT

In order to move ahead in your marriage, you need to know where you are. Go back to chapter 2 in *Divorce-Proof Your Marriage* and review your responses to the checklists for each of the stops on the marriage map. Then finish the exercise in the section "The State of Our Marriage." (Use the copies in appendix B.)

Do you truly believe that wherever you might be on the marriage map today, you can move back to the dream?

❏ Yes   ❏ No   ❏ I'm afraid to hope.

Gary and Barb say:

This is our message to you: No matter where you are on the marriage map—even if you are languishing in emotional divorce, even if you have initiated separation and legal divorce—good things are possible because a bond exists between you, and God will not let you ignore it. He created the marriage bond—that solemn covenant—to be unbreakable. Renewing love keeps it that way, helping you and your spouse feel confident and rooted in each other's love. (from introductory paragraphs in chapter 15)

In the book, you were given the opportunity to get back on the road and return to the dream. Below is the same exercise so that you can fill it out privately and then share it with your spouse in your Couple Interaction time.

Look at the list below, and check the loves that you feel will most effectively bring the growth your marriage needs. Then indicate in the blank to the right which love you feel deserves the highest priority in your strategy to get back on the road to the dream. Identify your top three priorities.

_____ Forgiving love (priority: _____)
_____ Serving love (priority: _____)
_____ Enduring love (priority: _____)
_____ Guarding love (priority: _____)
_____ Celebrating love (priority: _____)
_____ Renewing love (priority: _____)

Why did you rate them as you did?

_____

_____

_____

Pray for God's guidance as you seek to renew your commitment to your spouse.

Week Six—Day Two

COUPLE INTERACTION:
RENEWING THE COMMITMENT

Remember that during this week you need to read part 7—chapters 14 and 15 of *Divorce-Proof Your Marriage*.

1. If you have stashed away somewhere a videotape or audiotape of your wedding, pull it out and play it. Mainly, listen during the ceremony for the vows you made to each other. (If you have only photographs, get those out anyway and enjoy looking at them.) Then write the vows you said to each other:

    _____

    _____

    _____

2. When you think about the importance of such promises according to God's Word (God views promises as unbreakable), how should you view these words that you spoke to each other?

    _____

    _____

    _____

3. Share your answers to the questions from Day One.

4. Take your spouse's hands in yours, and once again speak the vows you said to each other so long ago.
    While still holding hands, pray together, asking God to renew your marriage.

Week Six—Day Three

MY ASSIGNMENT:
RENEWING THE COMMITMENT

You have two assignments this week:

1. Read part 7—chapters 14 and 15 of *Divorce-Proof Your Marriage*. Have you completed that assignment yet?

   ☐ Yes   ☐ No   ☐ I've started, but I have more to read.

My Journal

How did your Couple Interaction time go? Were there any insights or break-throughs? Explain.

_____

_____

_____

_____

_____

_____

_____

_____

_____

_____

Here is what I did and how it went when I practiced renewing love.

_____

_____

_____

_____

_____

_____

_____

_____

_____

Group Session Seven

NURTURE A RENEWING LOVE

SHARING AS A COUPLE

During the week, you and your spouse should have read part 7 of *Divorce-Proof Your Marriage*. Ideally you also made the time to work through the homework assignments so that you could discuss some aspects of renewing love and then begin to put them into practice!

As this session begins, couples should work together to answer the following questions:

1. What difference will it make in your marriage if you both make a decision that divorce is not an option, that you will keep your covenant promise that may have been along the lines of:

    for better or worse;
    for richer or poorer;
    in sickness and in health;
    to love and to cherish;
    till death do us part...

    _____

    _____

    _____

2. How would you like your marriage to be on your fiftieth wedding anniversary? Describe your vision for the two of you together at that time.

_____

_____

_____

REDISCOVERING RENEWING LOVE

Gary and Barb define renewing love as follows:

Renewing love refreshes and supports the marriage bond and helps spouses feel confident and rooted.

As a group, share some things you learned from reading the book or from your homework assignments about renewing love. Use the space below to write down anything that strikes you, any new ideas you have received, or new insights from others.

_____

_____

Why do marriages need renewing love? This is the love that allows your marriage to stay fresh—that allows you to keep learning wonderful new things about your spouse even after decades of marriage. Sure, a bouquet of cut roses is beautiful for a while, but because the flowers are not rooted, they will dry up and die. But a rose bush— planted, fertilized, and watered—will continue to bloom for years on end. Renewing love is like the rose bush. Have you ever seen an elderly couple walking together hand in hand? They spend time together, they talk, they laugh, they touch— even after fifty years of marriage. How can that happen? It happens with renewing love.

> *Gary and Barb say,*
> *Renewing love keeps the marriage commitment alive. It continually refreshes the solemn, heartfelt pledge of undying love we made to each other before God, our families, and our friends. What was that commitment about, really? It may seem like a silly question, but we know plenty of people who assume that their marriage commitment was simply about sexual fidelity or not ever getting divorced. But the marriage commitment is so much more than that. The real heart of renewing love is a commitment to keep growing together. It's an ongoing promise to love to the utmost of your ability—never to leave. It's a commitment sealed by the unbreakable bond God formed between you and your spouse when you made that one-of-a-kind promise. It's a living commitment powered by God.*
> (from chapter 14, under heading "Love That Goes the Distance")

3. The real heart of renewing love is a commitment to "keep growing together," but what does that mean? How can spouses grow together? Give as many ideas as you can below.

    _____

    _____

    _____

4. Gary and Barb offer some ideas for ways couples can develop renewing love. These are listed below (taken from chapter 14, under heading "Ways to Nurture Renewing Love"). After each is mentioned below, answer the accompanying question:

    How can couples decide to pursue their dream? What can they do to not leave their marriage to chance but to *decide* to make their marriage work?

    _____

    _____

    _____

    Why is commitment to Christ important for couples to truly be able to divorce-proof their marriages?

    _____

    _____

    _____

    _____

    How can spouse's enter each other's world? Why is that important?

    _____

    _____

    _____

    In what ways can a husband be a cheerleader for his wife? In what ways can a wife be a cheerleader for her husband?

    _____

    _____

    _____

Why is it important for couples to understand that when they said their vows, they were making a promise, a covenant? What does that mean? (More on this in question 5 below.)

_____

_____

_____

Why is it vital to agree that divorce is not an option?

_____

_____

_____

Marriages need renewing love in order to stay strong.

5. Marriage is a covenant. The dictionary defines a covenant as a "promise" or a "pledge." In the Bible, God made covenants with his people.

    "I solemnly promise never to send another flood to kill all living creatures and destroy the earth." And God said, "I am giving you a sign as evidence of my eternal covenant with you and all living creatures. I have placed my rainbow in the clouds. It is the sign of my permanent promise to you and to all the earth." (Genesis 9:11-13)

    He always stands by his covenant—the commitment he made to a thousand generations. (Psalm 105:8)

    Does God keep his covenants (promises)? Why does he do so?

    _____

    _____

    _____

    So when you make a promise to God, don't delay in following through, for God takes no pleasure in fools. Keep all the promises you make to him. It is better to say nothing than to promise something that you don't follow through on. In such cases, your mouth is making you sin. And don't defend yourself by telling the Temple messenger that the promise you made was a mistake. That would make God angry, and he might wipe out everything you have achieved. (Ecclesiastes 5:4-6)

Does God expect his followers to keep their covenants (promises)? Why?

_____

_____

_____

6. Why is it important for married couples to view their union as an unbreakable covenant? What difference would it make if more people would do that?

_____

_____

_____

Gary and Barb say,

Where you are in your marriage is important, but where you're headed is even more crucial. So Barb and I want to ask you a few other questions. What will you do to build the various kinds of divorce-proofing love into your marriage? Which kind of love do you most need today to begin divorce-proofing your marriage? Knowing that you can't tackle every problem at once—and that divorce-proofing is a lifelong process anyway—where are you and your spouse going to concentrate your efforts right now?
(from chapter 15, under heading "The Road Back to the Dream")

As a couple answer the question Gary and Barb put to you in the quotation above.

What will you do to build the various kinds of divorce-proofing love into your marriage?

_____

_____

_____

_____

Which kind of love do you most need today to begin divorce-proofing your marriage?

_____

_____

_____

_____

_____

Where are you and your spouse going to concentrate your efforts right now?

_____

_____

_____

PREPARING FOR THE WEEK

You have no homework assignments this week except to continue to discuss the things you've learned and to begin to put into practice the kind of divorce-proofing love that you both feel you need to concentrate on right now. You could also use this time to catch up on any missed assignments. Be prepared to come back next week for a special celebration! Your leader will be discussing with you how you want to do this celebration and may need your help with some aspects of the party.

Group Session Eight
A COVENANT CELEBRATION

This meeting is designed to be a closing, a "graduation," from the seven-week course you have just completed. You have learned a lot during these weeks that has given you invaluable help in divorce-proofing your marriage. Now you can "seal" this series with a commitment to each other to keep trying to put into practice what you have learned. (This is not a "renew your vows" ceremony. Instead, it is an opportunity to make a further commitment to your spouse to continue to work on these six kinds of love in your marriage.)

This will not be a regular meeting. This last session is planned to be a time of celebration for the couples in your group. This is a time for each couple to commit to continue practicing these six types of love in their marriages and a time to formally say that they want to divorce-proof their marriages.

At the back of this workbook is a copy of the certificate you and your spouse can sign as part of this graduation celebration. It reads as follows:

OUR COVENANT HOME
Together as husband and wife, we declare our home a divorce-proofed home—a covenant home—built on the solid foundation of Jesus Christ, characterized by unconditional love, and devoted to our lifelong commitment to each other.

By signing this covenant, we promise to

- Initiate a forgiving love when we've offended each other or when conflict arises.
- Demonstrate serving love by putting each other's needs above our own.
- Exercise persevering love by walking through the most difficult times—hand in hand.
- Establish a guarding love that will safeguard our marriage and let no man,

woman, or child divide us.
- Enjoy a celebrating love that keeps the spark alive in the relationship and celebrates you as my best friend.
- Experience a renewing love that says, "I'm committed to you until death do us part."

In the presence of God and these witnesses, and by a holy covenant, we promise to exhibit these loves towards each other every day. We promise that from this day forward, for better, for worse, for richer, for poorer, in sickness and in health, to forgive, to serve, to persevere, to guard, to celebrate, and to renew our love, forsaking all others as long as we both shall live.

Then there is a space for each of you to sign the document. If your group leader decides to prepare these in a special way, this document could be framed and placed in a prominent place in your home as a reminder—to you and to your children—of your commitment to divorce-proof your marriage.

Discover the Love of Your Life All Over Again

LEADER NOTES

Thank you for being willing to lead this study! We are so grateful to you for taking the time to take on what will be—we promise—an enjoyable and growing experience for you and a terrific experience for those who join you in this study. There is great reward in helping to strengthen Christian marriages. You've probably seen the devastation of divorce with friends, co-workers, and even in your own church. We want to help give spouses the tools to work on their marriages and to avoid ending up in divorce.

We hope that you're taking on this job because you're excited—you want to spread this message to as many people as you can! You see, in order to make these sessions work, you, the leader, need to be excited about the topic. You're going to need to motivate the married couples in your group to read the book and do their homework assignments. These are key. The homework is not a requirement, but stress to the couples that they will get so much more out of this time if they are willing to *make* the time to do these assignments during the week.

The Leader Notes that follow will provide you with:
- Answers for all of the fill-in-the-blanks in the workbook.
- Transition statements that you will read to the group at key points.
- Instructions for you to follow to help prepare for certain exercises and activities.

1. Order and distribute the following books to the couples before the first session so that they have time to do the required reading:
    - One copy of the book *Divorce-Proof Your Marriage* for **every couple** attending.

- One *Discover the Love of Your Life All Over Again* workbook for **every person** attending.

2. Contact all attendees a few days before the first session to remind them of the time and meeting location, and ask them to arrive at least ten minutes before the session starts. **Remind them to read part 1—chapters 1–3 in the *Divorce-Proof Your Marriage* book before the first group session.**

3. You will lead each session by reading the workbook lesson in its entirety. The participants will follow along in their workbooks and complete the exercises as you instruct. Use the additional comments and notes in these Leader Notes as you have the time.

4. Scripture passages are provided at appropriate times in the workbook. All passages are from the New Living Translation published by Tyndale House Publishers. This will make it easier for everyone to follow along from the same translation. You can have someone in the group read these passages, or you can read them to the group.

5. You will notice that each lesson suggests a question to be displayed as the group arrives. This is designed to help the group focus on the main idea of the lesson before you begin.

6. Begin each session with prayer. This entire study assumes that God has brought this group together. Consider the following when you pray:
   - We recognize that God brought every person to this study for a reason.
   - We are excited to discover new things about ourselves and our spouses.
   - We expect God to use his Holy Spirit to teach us how to become better servants to our spouses.
   - We give God the glory for the ways he will make our marriages better as we submit to his plan for us.

7. Consider how to help with child care. Perhaps your church youth group can help with this.

8. Room preparation:
   - Provide name tags, and ask attendees to prepare their name tag as they arrive.
   - Have a list of all attendees who signed up. Ask people to verify that their name is on the class sheet. Have someone at a table near the entrance to welcome each couple.

- If you are charging each couple for the books and workbooks, have someone at the table to collect the money for the books that have been distributed.
- Make sure you have adequate seating for everyone.
- Provide pens or pencils and extra Bibles for those who do not bring their own.

9. A note about the structure of this eight-week study: The first session is designed to introduce the couples to the broad idea of divorce-proofing their marriage. It will briefly review the six types of love that will be covered over the next six weeks. Sessions 2 through 7 then focus on each of the six kinds of love. Finally, session 8 is a celebration in which the couples can "graduate" and commit to working on their marriages.

Sharing as a Couple (This is a warm-up exercise for everyone, but it also allows couples who didn't get the homework done to get into the swing of what will be discussed.)

Rediscovering _____ Love (This provides a review of the material the couples will have read about in the book and worked on during the week.)

Preparing for the Week (Be sure to note the assignments and enthusiastically encourage the couples to read the book and do the homework assignments. If couples say that they just don't have the time, encourage them to *make* the time. It should take no more than thirty minutes to do the Couple Interaction section. They could do that discussion after dinner, before bed, etc. The point is, people don't *have* the time unless they *make* the time. If it is a priority, they should do it.)

10. Pray for your group members each week. Ask God to intervene with his Spirit to empower each couple to understand and meet each other's needs.

This study is designed as an introduction to the Divorce-Proofing America's Marriages campaign. This is the first in a series of workbook courses. This course will help couples renew their commitment and love for each other and come away with a deeper resolve to experience God's dream for their marriage. After this course, couples will be ready to learn how to live out each of the six loves and make them a more significant part of their relationship. There will be a book and a workbook for each of the six loves so couples can study each love more in depth. See the back of this book for information about these other products.

Leader Notes: Group Session One

PURSUE THE DREAM

LESSON PURPOSE

- To convince couples that God wants every marriage to be vibrant, growing, and exciting, and to realize that this dream is possible
- To introduce the six loves that will be studied in the coming sessions

LESSON FOCUS

In this session, couples will

- Discuss God's plan for every marriage.
- Consider the six different types of love to be presented in this study.
- Talk about how those six types of love are needed in every marriage.

LESSON PREPARATION

Post this question so it can be seen by everyone who enters the room:

**What hopes and dreams did you have for
your marriage on your wedding day?**

LESSON PLAN

Begin with prayer.

INTRODUCTION

Spend five minutes briefly touching on the material contained in the Introduction—How to Use This Book section of the workbook. Discuss the focus and goals of this course as described in the Introduction, and make sure everyone understands the three days of homework that each couple is to complete during the week between each group session.

Read aloud the introduction of Group Session One. Give the group members a bit of time to answer the questions about how they met their spouse and what it was that drew them to each other. Then ask if anyone would like to share his or her answers.

Transition:

"All of us began our marriage with some preconceived idea of what we wanted our marriage to be like. Some of us could picture the image of a man and woman who were best friends and fell deeply in love. Others had the idea of raising children and growing old together. Some of us had only a vague idea of what we wanted from our marriage. But did you know that God had a dream for your marriage?"

[Ask someone to read aloud the Bible passage from Genesis in the workbook. Then walk through questions 1-3.]

Transition:

"Marriage is not a single event. Rather, it is a process that begins with a single event: the wedding. From that point forward, we are committed to working together to fulfill God's plan. We will call this process a journey. The Rosbergs have learned that there is a map for this journey, which they call the marriage map (see in back of workbook or book). You read about this in chapter 2 of your book. (If you have not yet read the first three chapters, please do so this week. You also will want to answer the questions there.) During this course, we will examine six types of love that are necessary to prevent a marriage from drifting away from the dream God has for you and your spouse."

[Together as a group, work on question 4. Read through the definitions of each type of love. You as the leader will give the words that fill in the blanks (see below) and ask the group members to write those words in the spaces. After each type of love is defined, take a few minutes to discuss why that type of love is needed in a marriage.]

FORGIVING LOVE

Forgiving love offers a <u>fresh</u> <u>start</u> after you have <u>offended</u> and <u>hurt</u> each other. Forgiving love equips you to <u>communicate</u> on such a <u>deep</u> level of acceptance for one another that you can <u>recover</u> from the <u>pain</u> you occasionally <u>inflict</u> on one another and <u>work</u> through your offenses. Forgiving love helps you to <u>reconnect</u> after you have <u>hurt</u> one another.

Every marriage needs forgiving love because . . .

SERVING LOVE

Serving love helps you <u>discover</u> and <u>meet</u> each other's deepest <u>needs.</u> Serving love is the process of <u>identifying</u> needs and taking steps to <u>meet</u> them in each other.

Every marriage needs serving love because . . .

PERSEVERING LOVE

Persevering love <u>sustains</u> you through the <u>trials</u> of life. As you implement persevering love in your marriage, you will <u>bond</u> with your spouse and <u>enjoy</u> a love that will <u>persevere</u> through your years together.

Every marriage needs persevering love because . . .

GUARDING LOVE

Guarding love <u>protects</u> your <u>hearts</u> from <u>threats</u> to your marriage. Marriages are <u>threatened</u> by many forces today. If you are not aware of the <u>threats</u> to your marriage, then you are <u>vulnerable.</u>

Every marriage needs guarding love because . . .

CELEBRATING LOVE

Celebrating love <u>equips</u> you to maintain a satisfying <u>emotional, physical,</u> and <u>spiritual</u> connection. Celebrating love keeps that <u>spark</u> alive, not only in the bedroom but in all areas of the <u>relationship.</u> As you learn to celebrate your <u>oneness,</u> you will fall in love all over again.

Every marriage needs celebrating love because . . .

RENEWING LOVE

Renewing love regards the marriage <u>covenant</u> as <u>unbreakable.</u> Renewing love <u>protects</u> you from <u>insecurity</u> and provides you with <u>confident</u> <u>assurance</u> as you face your future with your spouse.

Every marriage needs renewing love because . . .

[Read the quote from Gary and Barb.]

SHARING AS A COUPLE

Have the couples spend a few minutes together answering question 5 and filling in the chart.

PREPARING FOR THE WEEK

Read through the workbook section that describes some ground rules for the group session and the homework. Briefly explain that the group members are to read part 2—chapters 4 and 5 in the *Divorce-Proof Your Marriage* book—and then complete the three homework assignments that call for individual reflection as well as working together as a couple. This week will introduce the concept of forgiving love.

End the meeting in prayer.

Leader Notes: Group Session Two

FORGIVE AND FORGET

LESSON PURPOSE

- To review forgiving love and how the couples were able to practice forgiveness during the past week
- To discuss what it really means to forgive

LESSON FOCUS

In this session, couples will

- Review the biblical steps to being able to act on forgiving love.
- Consider what obstacles to forgiveness they may be facing in their marriages.

LESSON PREPARATION

Post this question so it can be seen by everyone who enters the room:

Have you ever needed to be forgiven?

LESSON PLAN

Begin with prayer.

SHARING AS A COUPLE

Spend a few minutes allowing couples to talk together and answer questions 1 and 2. Encourage them to be honest, and remind them that they will not be asked to share their answers with anyone else.

Transition:

"I hope that you made the time to read the chapters in your book and work through the three homework assignments. I really encourage you to do this every week. You will get so much more out of this entire study if you make the time. We will spend each session reviewing the material you read in the book over the last week and discussing any questions that may have arisen as you did the homework. There will be opportunity for you to share some experiences or insights you may have had as you worked on this particular love during the last week."

REDISCOVERING FORGIVING LOVE

Read aloud the material in the workbook, and then ask the group to share any thoughts, ideas, insights, or questions that may have come up during their reading and homework assignments during the past week.

> *[Read Gary and Barb's quote and the introductory paragraph about the myths of forgiveness. The answers to the blanks are below.]*

Some myths surrounding forgiveness:

Myth #1: "When I forgive, I must also <u>forget</u>."
   (The Bible never says we must forget the offenses.)

Myth #2: "The <u>hurt</u> is too great. It is <u>impossible</u> for me to forgive."
   (God would never command us to do something we cannot do.)

Myth #3: "I don't <u>feel</u> like forgiving, so my forgiveness can't be <u>genuine</u>."
   (Forgiveness is a choice, not a feeling.)

Myth #4: "I <u>can't</u> forgive unless the other person <u>asks</u> for it."
   (We must forgive without conditions.)

Myth #5: "In order to forgive, I must <u>pretend</u> that <u>nothing</u> bad happened."
   (If you have to forgive, then something happened. We are not to pretend.)

Myth #6: "I must forgive <u>right away</u> or it <u>doesn't count</u>."
   (We are not to let anger fester, but we should be realistic.)

> *[Review the forgiveness "loop," and make sure it makes sense. Then read the quote from Gary and Barb in the workbook before moving on to question 3.*

*Either be prepared to read the Bible verses noted in the workbook, or have
someone ready to read them. Then you as the leader will give the words that
fill in the blanks (see below) and ask the group members to write those
words in the spaces. After each step, discuss why that step is important in
the process of forgiveness.]*

Step 1: Prepare Your Heart

Read Philippians 2:3-5.

To prepare my heart, I need to <u>humble</u> myself and <u>pray.</u> That way, I'll be more
able to see my spouse's <u>perspective.</u> Then, I should look for the <u>underlying</u> <u>cause</u>
of the conflict to truly understand what has <u>angered</u> me. I will <u>commit</u> to making
my relationship with my spouse my <u>top</u> <u>priority</u>.

In order to forgive, I need to prepare my heart because . . .

Step 2: Communicate Your Feelings

Read James 1:19.

To communicate my feelings, I will <u>think</u> <u>ahead</u> about what I want to say so that
I don't spout off with hurtful words. I will speak <u>kindly</u> and <u>calmly,</u> and then I
will <u>listen.</u> I will try to be <u>positive</u>, say what I mean, and not speak in <u>generaliza-</u>
<u>tions</u>. I will communicate <u>openly</u> and <u>honestly</u>.

In order to forgive, I need to communicate my feelings because . . .

Step 3: Confront Your Conflicts

Read Ephesians 4:26-27.

My spouse and I are not <u>adversaries</u>; we are on the same <u>team</u>. By working
<u>together</u>, we can find a <u>solution</u>. To do this we will <u>choose</u> an <u>appropriate</u> <u>time</u>
and <u>setting</u> to discuss our conflict. We will find out if we are <u>ready</u> to discuss the
issue. I will not assign <u>blame.</u> This kind of <u>loving</u> <u>confrontation</u> will help us close
the loop.

In order to forgive, I need to confront the conflict because . . .

Step 4: Forgive Your Spouse

Read Mark 11:24-25.

Now the rubber meets the road. I not only must forgive, but I must <u>act</u> out forgiveness. I may have to <u>request</u> forgiveness, or I may have to <u>grant</u> forgiveness.
The ability to <u>let</u> <u>go</u> of past hurts is perhaps the single most <u>important</u> relationship <u>skill</u> we can develop in our marriage.

In order to forgive, I need to act out forgiveness because . . .

Step 5: Rebuild Your Trust

Read 2 Corinthians 5:17-19.

<u>Trust</u> isn't rebuilt <u>overnight</u>. Yet through the power of <u>Christ's</u> redeeming love, our marriage can be <u>transformed</u> from <u>rubble</u> to <u>restoration.</u>

In order to forgive, I need to work to rebuild trust because . . .

Transition:

Ask: "Why are these steps important in being able to experience forgiving love in a marriage? What happens if any of these steps are skipped?"

[Give the group members a few minutes to individually consider and answer question 4.]

PREPARING FOR THE WEEK

Remind group members to read part 3—chapters 6 and 7 in *Divorce-Proof Your Marriage* during the coming week and to complete their three homework pages. Remind them that the way they can best gain a lot out of this session is to stay caught up on the reading and to work on the homework both individually and together. Also remind the group of the rules laid down in the first session regarding confidentiality among the group members regarding anything that is shared in the session. This week will introduce the concept of serving love.

End the meeting in prayer.

Leader Notes: Group Session Three

THE PLACE OF SERVICE

LESSON PURPOSE

- To review serving love and how the couples were able to serve
- To think about what it means to meet one another's needs

LESSON FOCUS

In this session, couples will

- Consider the biblical qualities of servanthood.
- Discover why communication is vital for spouses to be able to love each other with serving love.
- Look at different levels of communication and consider how they might be able to improve in communicating.

LESSON PREPARATION

Post this question so it can be seen by everyone who enters the room:

How does it feel to be honored?

LESSON PLAN

Begin with prayer.

Sharing as a Couple
Spend a few minutes allowing couples to talk together and answer questions 1, 2, and 3.

Transition:
"As difficult as it may be to comprehend, God expects of us what was also expected of Christ. Note that Jesus is our example of servanthood, and you saw a facet of that attitude in the reading you just did with your spouse. You might feel as if you could never exhibit this kind of love, and you are right. On your own, this is impossible. But where we fail, God succeeds. Let's consider how this servant love will safeguard a marriage and move it closer to the dream."

Rediscovering Serving Love
Read aloud the material in the workbook, and then ask the group to share any thoughts, ideas, insights, or questions that may have come up during their reading and homework assignments during the past week.

> *[Ask someone to read aloud Romans 12:10, and then work together to answer question 4.]*

> *[Read aloud the quote from Gary and Barb, and work with the group to answer question 5. Then ask someone to read the Philippians passage, and work as a group to answer question 6.]*

> *[Read aloud the quote from Gary and Barb, and then have each person individually answer question 7. Work together as a group on question 8. For question 9, the answers to the blanks are below. After each type of communication, discuss some examples—especially in marriage.]*

Sharing General Information
We speak largely in <u>clichés.</u>
Examples:

Sharing Facts
We discuss <u>people</u> and <u>events,</u> but nothing <u>personal.</u>
Examples:

Sharing Opinions and Beliefs
We share <u>personal</u> <u>information,</u> but nothing too <u>risky.</u>
Examples:

Sharing Feelings and Emotions
> We begin to <u>open</u> our <u>hearts.</u>
> Examples:

Sharing Needs, Intimate Concerns, Hopes, and Fears
> We <u>vulnerably</u> share our <u>heart</u> of hearts.
> Examples:

PREPARING FOR THE WEEK

Remind group members to read part 4—chapters 8 and 9 of *Divorce-Proof Your Marriage* during the coming week and to complete their three homework assignments. Sometimes it is the very difficulties in life that keep couples from having the energy to work on their marriage—but that's what persevering love is all about. Persevering love will be introduced this week. Challenge the group to stick with it and to view the time they spend working on this study as an investment in their most important account—their marriage.

End the meeting in prayer.

Leader Notes: Group Session Four

GROWING THROUGH TRIALS

LESSON PURPOSE

- To review persevering love and how the couples were able to practice persevering love during the past week
- To consider what it means to keep the vow of loving through "better or worse"

LESSON FOCUS

In this session, couples will
- Consider God's example of persevering love.
- Lay the "bricks" of the foundation for persevering love.

LESSON PREPARATION

Post this question so it can be seen by everyone who enters the room:

What has been the most difficult test of your marriage?

LESSON PLAN

Begin with prayer.

SHARING AS A COUPLE
Spend a few minutes allowing couples to talk together and answer questions 1, 2, and 3.

Transition:
"During this week you've been studying about the qualities of persevering love. Perhaps you are going through a trial right now that is having a significant impact on your marriage. Or maybe the trials you are facing today do not threaten your marriage, but they are making your marriage more difficult and stressful.

"Regardless of your present circumstance, you will face trials that can threaten your marriage. Even if you would never consider divorce, trials can move you away from God's dream for your marriage and toward emotional divorce.

"God would never ask us to do something he himself would not do. Let's talk about the definition of persevering love, and examine how the Bible describes God's persevering love for us."

REDISCOVERING PERSEVERING LOVE
Read aloud the material in the workbook, and then ask the group to share any thoughts, ideas, insights, or questions that may have come up during their reading and homework assignments during the past week.

> [Read the quote from Gary and Barb. Do question 4 as a group. Have different people read each Bible verse aloud, and then together write on the lines the characteristics of God's persevering love.]

> [Read aloud the quote from Gary and Barb, and then move on to question 5. The answers to the blanks are below. After each "brick," discuss the questions as a group.]

Brick #1: Connect and Stay Connected
Your ability to <u>endure</u> together in the hard times is directly <u>proportional</u> to the <u>depth</u> of your <u>partnership</u> in good times. To stay glued together in <u>difficulties,</u> you have to apply the cement of partnership in the <u>good</u> times.

Ideas for how spouses can connect . . .

Brick #2: Make Your Relationship a Safe Place
Your spouse needs to know that your <u>loving arms</u> will always be a <u>shelter</u> in the midst of a <u>trial</u> or <u>tragedy.</u>

When might spouses need a "safe place" in their marriage?

Brick #3: Keep Communicating

Trials can drive a <u>wedge</u> between a husband and wife. It is important to communicate and be the best <u>help</u> you can be.

In what ways do trials drive a wedge between spouses?

Brick #4: Rest in the Truth That God Has a Purpose for Trials

Great marriages are often forged through <u>difficult</u> <u>trials</u>. Acknowledge that God has a <u>purpose</u> in the trials to build your <u>character.</u>

How can spouses hang on to the truth of God's purpose in their trial?

Brick #5: Decide to Tackle Trouble Together—Wherever It Takes You

When you commit to this level of <u>persevering</u> <u>love</u>, you are offering your spouse the <u>assurance</u> that he or she will never be <u>alone</u> when <u>trials</u> come.

PREPARING FOR THE WEEK

Remind group members to read part 5—chapters 10 and 11 of *Divorce-Proof Your Marriage* during the coming week and to complete their three homework pages. This week will introduce the concept of guarding love.

End the meeting in prayer.

Leader Notes: Group Session Five

DEFEAT THE ENEMIES AT THE GATE

LESSON PURPOSE

- To review guarding love and what it means to guard one's heart
- To discuss how the couples were able to guard their marriages and their hearts during the past week

LESSON FOCUS

In this session, couples will

- Discuss why guarding love is important—even if you don't think you would ever be at risk
- Work in separate groups to explore how to guard their spouses' hearts.

LESSON PREPARATION

Post this question so it can be seen by everyone who enters the room:

In what ways are you guarding your heart?

LESSON PLAN

Begin with prayer.

SHARING AS A COUPLE

Spend a few minutes allowing couples to talk together and answer questions 1, 2, and 3.

Transition:

"Today we are going to discuss guarding love. You may feel as if this is a lesson you don't need. You may think, *I'll never have this problem. I'll never be tempted away by anything. So I'll just half listen to this lesson.* Maybe you didn't even read the chapters in the book because you thought this was a lesson you could skip. Well, let's set aside all of that wishful thinking. While it may very well be true that you wouldn't be tempted, you need to understand that you're guarding your heart against all kinds of intruders into your marriage—not just other people who might try to intrude. The best way to protect your marriage is to diligently guard it."

REDISCOVERING GUARDING LOVE

Read aloud the definition of guarding love, and then ask the group to share any thoughts, ideas, insights, or questions that may have come up during their reading and homework assignments during the past week.

> *[Discuss with the group why it is important to guard their marriages. They could share their answers from question 3. Then read aloud the material in the book. The answers to the blanks in question 4 are below.]*

The instruction to "guard your heart" means to <u>purposely</u> place a <u>protective shield</u> around the center of your life. You need to post a <u>watch</u> and exercise great <u>care.</u> When you guard your heart, you are guarding all that is truly <u>valuable</u> in life. It will protect your marriage from both <u>internal</u> and <u>external</u> threats.

> *[Read the quote from Gary and Barb.]*

Transition:

"Imagine that your marriage is like a castle. Surrounding it are vast walls and complexes with one purpose: to protect what lies within. If you've ever seen castles in Great Britain, you know that the people in those countries were masters at building castles. They had to for their very survival.

"The first thing you learn about a castle is that the most vulnerable part is the gate. Therefore, the gate was the most fortified and guarded place in the castle. In fact, castles have what is called a gatehouse. This is the complex of towers, bridges, and barriers built just to protect the gate itself. The better the protection surrounding the gate, the more secure the inhabitants felt.

"For all of us in this study, the gate to our marriage is our heart. As you are vigilant and dedicated to protect this gate, your marriage is safe. But if you drop your guard or fail to ensure the quality of your heart, your marriage becomes at best inse-cure, and at worst it will be destroyed. That's why guarding love is so important in your marriage."

> *[Divide the group into two groups, one of men and one of women. The women should talk together and answer the questions in the section called "For the Women," while the men talk together and answer the questions in the section called "For the Men." After several minutes, bring the group back together and read the last quote from Gary and Barb.]*

PREPARING FOR THE WEEK
Remind group members to read part 6—chapters 12 and 13 of *Divorce-Proof Your Marriage* during the coming week and to complete their three homework pages. This week will introduce the concept of celebrating love.

End the meeting in prayer.

CELEBRATE WHAT GOD HAS GIVEN

LESSON PURPOSE

- To review celebrating love and how the couples were able to celebrate their marriages during the past week
- To offer ideas for helping couples keep alive the celebration and joy of their marriage

LESSON FOCUS

In this session, couples will
- Talk about celebrating love and the importance of spiritual intimacy.
- Consider how spiritual intimacy will help them live out all of the types of love discussed in these sessions.

LESSON PREPARATION

Post this question so it can be seen by everyone who enters the room:

How can you celebrate your love?

LESSON PLAN

Begin with prayer.

SHARING AS A COUPLE

Spend a few minutes allowing couples to talk together and answer questions 1 and 2.

Transition:

"Our goal for this session is to motivate you to celebrate your relationship. If you adopt this love for your marriage, you will learn a way of loving that will protect you and your spouse from drifting apart. Celebration sounds like fun, but all too often it gets set aside in the humdrum or the worries of everyday married life."

REDISCOVERING CELEBRATING LOVE

Read aloud the material in the workbook, along with the definition of celebrating love, and ask the group to share any thoughts, ideas, insights, or questions that may have come up during their reading and homework assignments during the past week.

> *[Read the paragraph about celebration, and then work as a group on question 3. The answers to fill in the blanks are below.]*

Put Each Other at the Top of the List

The first key to celebrating love is to move each other to the <u>top</u> of your <u>to-do</u> list. You need <u>quantity</u> time. Find <u>enjoyable</u> <u>activities</u> to do together. Don't give each other <u>leftover</u> time.

Confess to Each Other

<u>Unresolved</u> <u>offenses</u> block all kinds of intimacy. Close the <u>forgiveness</u> <u>loop</u> when you sense a <u>wall</u> between you and your spouse.

Get to Know Each Other Again

Demonstrate your <u>love</u> by showing that you are <u>deeply</u> <u>interested</u> in your spouse. Rediscover each other's <u>strengths,</u> <u>personal</u> <u>interests,</u> and <u>uniqueness.</u>

Rethink Your Thinking

Ask God to <u>refresh</u> your <u>love</u> for your spouse. Be willing to <u>fall</u> <u>in</u> <u>love</u> with your spouse all over again.

Rekindle Romance and Physical Intimacy

Both spouses need to understand the different <u>intimacy</u> needs they have. Women need to <u>talk</u> and have <u>emotional</u> <u>intimacy;</u> for men, intimacy is found in the <u>sexual</u> <u>relationship.</u>

> *[Lead the group through the rest of the questions in the session, stopping to read the quotations or material in the book when appropriate.]*

PREPARING FOR THE WEEK

Remind group member to read part 7—chapters 14 and 15 of *Divorce-Proof Your Marriage* during the coming week and to complete their three homework assignments. This week will introduce the concept of renewing love.

End the meeting in prayer.

Leader Notes: Group Session Seven

NURTURE A RENEWING LOVE

LESSON PURPOSE

- To discuss the concept of renewing love and what it means to see marriage as a covenant before God
- To develop a vision for how a marriage can look after fifty years

LESSON FOCUS

In this session, couples will

- Consider some keys to renewing love and talk about how they can develop those in their marriages.
- Examine the biblical concept of "covenant."
- Talk about where to go from here.

LESSON PREPARATION

Post this question so it can be seen by everyone who enters the room:

What makes you feel confident and rooted in your marriage?

LESSON PLAN

Begin with prayer.

SHARING AS A COUPLE
Spend a few minutes allowing couples to talk together and answer questions 1 and 2.

Transition:
"I hope that you made the time to read the chapters in your book and work through the three homework assignments. Those of you who have faithfully kept up, congratulations! I'm sure you can say that you've learned some new things and deepened your relationship already. Some of you may have had a couple weeks where getting together to talk just didn't happen. We still hope you've been able to discover some new ideas through these session. You should make an effort to finish reading the book. We would also like you to make some time together to discuss things that are vital to your own marriage. Today we're discussing the last love in the book—renewing love. Although this is the last one, it is by no means the least important. In fact, all of these loves are equally important—although some may be more needed than others in your particular marriage. With renewing love, Gary and Barb even say that if you want a rock-solid commitment, start here because this kind of love sets all the others in motion."

REDISCOVERING RENEWING LOVE
Read aloud the material in the workbook, along with the definition of renewing love, and ask the group to share any thoughts, ideas, insights, or questions that may have come up during their reading and homework assignments during the past week.

[Read the paragraph about renewing love, and then the quote from Gary and Barb. Work as a group to answer question 3.]

[Note that question 4 has several parts, and each part corresponds to the sections under the heading "Ways to Nurture Renewing Love" in chapter 14. You may need to have your book open to help jump-start some ideas. Ask the group to answer the questions in the workbook together, and give ideas and examples where appropriate.]

[Question 5 begins a quick study of how God views covenants. Make sure your group understands that when they said their vows to each other on their wedding day, they were making a covenant. Read, or ask someone to read, the passages in the book, and then answer the questions.]

[Work as a group to answer question 6, and then read the quote from Gary and Barb. The last quote comprises the final challenge to the lesson. Your group needs to know that they should continue to work on divorce-proofing their marriages for the rest of their lives. Ask each husband and wife to form a couple group and answer the last three questions in the workbook about what actions they will take from here on.]

Preparing for the Week

Explain to your group that there is no homework this week, unless of course they want to catch up on anything they missed during the session. Next week will be a special celebration, a "graduation" of sorts. They will have the opportunity to sign the marriage covenant (see the back of this book for an example). You may want to plan to have food, so talk with the group about how you want to handle this—eat out, bring food, be catered, etc. If you decide to make a "wedding celebration" complete with cake, decide how you will get the cake—have someone make it, buy something suitable at the bakery, etc. You will need to provide for utensils and drinks as well. Enlist group members to help. Some groups have even brought children along to this celebration to take part in their parents' desire to divorce-proof their marriage. This is all for your group to decide.

You will also need to prepare the "Our Covenant Home" certificates from appendix C. You can photocopy these on nice paper, or design your own. If you would like color versions of this certificate, you can download them from our Web site: www.divorceproof.com. You may also want to prepare the churchwide covenant certificate that everyone will sign. For more information, see the Leader Notes for session 8.

Leader Notes: Group Session Eight

A COVENANT CELEBRATION

SUGGESTED FORMAT

WELCOME

Thank the couples for the commitment they have exhibited over the last seven weeks to study the book, attend the meetings, and work on the homework assignments. Remind them that they are part of a nationwide movement and that many groups across the country are doing just what they are doing—studying how to keep their marriages strong in a day when marriage is under heavy attack. You could say something like:

> Thank you so much for all your hard work these last seven weeks. I think you'll agree with me that this has been well worth it. If you began this series already in a great place on the marriage map, I hope that you have discovered some tools to keep your marriage strong. If you began this series in a difficult place in your marriage, I hope that you have gained some insights and ideas that will bring you both closer together and walk you back up the marriage map to a place of strength. I hope that you've discovered ways to divorce-proof your marriage.
>
> There is a movement afoot in this country to literally take back America's marriages. Groups just like ours all over the country are meeting in churches, in homes, in Sunday school classes to learn how to strengthen their marriages. With Christian marriages heading for divorce court just as often as non-Christian marriages, obviously something has gone wrong. And the only way to stop such a trend in its tracks is to hit it head on. After all,

if we as a church don't take a stand, who will? If it doesn't start here, then where?

The series you have just completed and the book you've read, *Divorce-Proof Your Marriage,* is an overview of the six types of love that every marriage needs in order to stay strong. I'd like you to note that Gary and Barbara Rosberg are writing separate books that delve more deeply into each of these six loves, and then there are workbooks for those as well. So we have only begun to scratch the surface of this issue. If you want to do more, talk to me afterward. There are more tools available so that you can study each of these loves more in depth.

RECAP OF THE COURSE
Any good series needs a good review. Take a few minutes to remind the group of the definitions of the six loves they have studied:

During these past weeks we've been studying six principles of divorce-proofing our marriages and then putting them into practice in our homes. We are doing it for the sake of our marriages and for the sake of the next generation. We've talked about six different kinds of love that are vital to every marriage relationship. These include:

● *Forgiving love,* that heals hurts and helps us feel accepted by and connected to each other;

● *Serving love* that discovers and meets needs and helps us feel honored and understood.

● *Persevering love* that stays strong in tough times and helps us feel bonded—best friends for life.

● *Guarding love* that protects from threats and helps us feel safe and secure.

● *Celebrating love* that rejoices in the marriage relationship and helps us feel cherished and captivated.

● *Renewing love* that refreshes and supports the marriage bond and helps us feel confident and rooted.

EXPLANATION OF THE COVENANT
Explain the significance of the word "covenant":

Today (tonight) we are gathering to sign our marriage covenant documents. The Marriage Covenant reads: [read aloud the covenant as it appears on the document the couples will sign].

The word *covenant* isn't a term we use much anymore, but it's a very important word. A covenant is a binding, unbreakable agreement between two parties. We find several covenants in the Bible, for God made covenants with people. For example:

❑ God made a covenant with Abraham when he promised to make his descendants a mighty people;

❑ God made a covenant with Moses and the Israelites when he gave them the Ten Commandments;

❑ God made a covenant with David when he swore that his throne would last forever; and

❑ God made a covenant with us when Christ died for our sins and opened our way to God through faith in him.

Can you sense that a covenant is a serious thing? When you affirmed your commitment to each other by saying vows on a very special day years ago, those vows were a promise, a covenant. Marriage is entered into by covenant.

A commitment that is lived out daily is what gives marriages confidence and security. We don't need to peer into the future and wonder whether we are staying together or not. We can know for certain ahead of time what the choice will be. Covenant commitment gives us the ability to confidently say, "We're going to persevere. We're going to make it. We're going to paddle upstream in a culture that doesn't applaud commitment."

Husbands and wives, the very survival of our marriages depends on our recognition of the covenant we made on our wedding day. To have a renewing love is to be able to say with absolute conviction: "Divorce is not an option. We are married for life."

BIBLE PASSAGE
Read Malachi 2:10-16. The passage is quoted from the New Living Translation below:

Are we not all children of the same Father? Are we not all created by the same God? Then why are we faithless to each other, violating the covenant of our ancestors? In Judah, in Israel, and in Jerusalem there is treachery, for the men of Judah have defiled the Lord's beloved sanctuary by marrying women who worship idols. May the Lord cut off from the nation of Israel every last man who has done this and yet brings an offering to the Lord Almighty. Here is another thing you do. You cover the Lord's altar with tears, weeping and groaning because he pays no attention to your offerings, and he doesn't accept them with pleasure. You cry out, "Why has the Lord abandoned us?" I'll tell you why! Because the Lord witnessed the vows you and your wife made to each other on your wedding day when you were young. But you have been disloyal to her, though she remained your faithful companion, the wife of your marriage vows. Didn't the Lord make you one with your wife? In body and spirit you are his. And what does he want? Godly children from your union. So guard yourself; remain loyal to the wife of your youth. "For I hate divorce!" says the Lord, the God of Israel. "It is as cruel as putting on a victim's bloodstained coat," says the Lord Almighty. "So guard yourself; always remain loyal to your wife."

Clearly, God does not take divorce lightly. In fact, he says in no uncertain terms, "I hate divorce!" The passage tells us that God witnessed the vows that we made to each other on our wedding day. When we said those vows and made that commitment, God made us one with our spouse. What does God expect from us? To keep our promise; to keep our covenant; to remain loyal to each other. We are to guard ourselves and always remain loyal—wives to husbands, and husbands to wives. The covenant goes beyond just the married couple, however. God wants us to remain committed for the sake of the next generation.

RECITING THE COMMITMENT

Ask the spouses to turn to each other and hold hands. Ask the husbands to repeat after you the statement that you will read from the marriage covenant:

By signing this covenant, I promise to:

- Initiate a forgiving love when I've been offended or when conflict arises.

- Demonstrate serving love by putting your needs above my own.

- Exercise persevering love by walking through the most difficult times with you—hand in hand.

- Establish a guarding love that will safeguard our marriage and let no man, woman, or child divide us.

- Enjoy a celebrating love that keeps the spark alive in our relationship and celebrates you as my best friend.

- Experience a renewing love that says, "I'm committed to you until death do us part."

Then ask the wives to repeat the same statement to their husbands.

Prayer
Lead the couples in prayer.

Kiss
What would any such ceremony be without "the kiss"?

Signing the Covenant
Have the couples come forward to sign their own personal certificates. These can be downloaded from our Web site (www.divorceproof.com) or you can create your own by using the template in appendix C at the back of this workbook. You may also want to prepare a churchwide covenant for all couples to sign. This could be displayed in the church hallway and added onto with additional years of divorce-proofing couples. This adds to the church community a "we" mind-set.

Closing
Have everyone stand, and give the following blessing to the couples:

> You have made a very important covenant before God. You have chosen your marriage—against all odds. You know that your spouse isn't perfect—and you know that you aren't either. You have already been through much together. And you've made a commitment to keep going.

> Put on the armor God offers you. Take the Word of God into your heart and into your home. Stay on your knees in prayer. Stay clean before each other and before your Lord Jesus Christ. Experience God's grace and forgiveness each new day. When it gets tough, remember your commitment before God. Remember what you have learned about love, and keep on going—together.

> God bless you.

RECEPTION

Adjourn to the reception.

APPENDICES

CAMPAIGN RESOURCES FOR DIVORCE-PROOFING AMERICA'S MARRIAGES

Dear friends,

The resources for the Divorce-Proofing America's Marriages campaign are designed *for you*—to help you divorce-proof your marriage. You and your spouse can certainly read and study these books as a couple. But it's only when you meet with a small group that is committed to divorce-proofing their marriages as well that you'll fully experience the power of these ideas. There's power when believers unite in a common cause. There's power when men and women keep each other accountable. To take on this challenge, you must have a group of friends who are encouraging you every step of the way.

There are several ways you can connect to a small group:

- Start your own Divorce-Proofing America's Marriages small group in your church or neighborhood. For workbooks, leader's guides, videos, and other resources for your small group, call 888-ROSBERG (888-767-2374) or visit our Web site at **www.divorceproof.com**.

- Give this information to your pastor or elders at your local church. They may want to host a Divorce-Proofing America's Marriages small group in your church.

- Call America's Family Coaches at 888-ROSBERG (888-767-2374), or e-mail us at afc@afclive.com and we will connect you with people and churches who are interested in Divorce-Proofing America's Marriages.

Yes, together we can launch a nationwide campaign and see countless homes transformed into covenant homes. But beware. If we do not teach these principles to our own children, we risk missing the greatest opportunity of all: to pass our legacy of godly homes to the next generation. Barb and I believe that, *for the sake of the next generation,* there is no more worthy cause. This holy fire must purify our own homes first.

Gary and Barb Rosberg

DIVORCE-PROOF YOUR MARRIAGE
ISBN 0-8423-4995-2
Audio CD (3 CDs) ISBN 0-8423-6592-3
Audiocassette (2 cassettes) ISBN 0-8423-6894-9

DISCOVER THE LOVE OF YOUR LIFE ALL OVER AGAIN (workbook)
ISBN 0-8423-7342-X

Your house is weatherproofed. But is your marriage divorce-proofed? In this foundational book of the Divorce-Proofing America's Marriages campaign, Gary and Barb show couples how to keep their marriages safe from the threat of divorce. Divorce doesn't happen suddenly. Over months and years couples can slide from the dream to disappointment and eventually to emotional divorce. However, they can stop the slide by learning to love in six unique ways. Small groups will enjoy the *Discover the Love of Your Life All Over Again* workbook, which includes eight sessions. Together couples will practice healing hurt in their marriages, meeting their spouses' needs, strengthening each other through difficult times, guarding their marriage against threats, celebrating their spouses, and renewing their love for each other day after day. A weekly devotion and assignment will help couples practice what they learn in the context of the encouragement of couples who are committed to the same goal of divorce-proofing their marriages. This workbook includes an easy-to-follow leader's guide.

THE 5 LOVE NEEDS OF MEN AND WOMEN
ISBN 0-8423-4239-7
Audiocassette (2 cassettes) ISBN 0-8423-3587-0

SERVING LOVE (workbook)
ISBN 0-8423-7343-8

You, too, can learn how to become your spouse's best friend with *The Five Love Needs of Men and Women* book and workbook. In this book, Gary talks to women about the deepest needs of their husbands, and Barb talks to men about the most intimate needs of their wives. You'll discover the deep yearnings of your spouse. And when you join a group studying the *Serving Love* workbook, you will learn how to understand and meet your spouse's needs within a circle of encouraging friends. They can help you find ways to meet those needs day after day, week after week. The workbook includes eight group sessions, three weekly activities, and ideas for a date night with your spouse. Easy-to-follow leader's guide included.

40 UNFORGETTABLE DATES WITH YOUR MATE
ISBN 0-8423-6106-5

When's the last time you and your spouse went on an unforgettable date? Saying "I do" certainly doesn't mean you're finished working at your marriage. Nobody ever put a tank of gas in a car and expected it to run for years. But lots of couples are running on emotional fumes of long-ago dates. Truth is, if you're not dating your spouse, your relationship is not growing. Bring the zing back into your marriage with *40 Unforgettable Dates with Your Mate,* a book that gives husbands and wives ideas on how they can meet the five love needs of their spouse. Wives, get the inside scoop on your husband. Men, discover what your wife finds irresistible. Gary and Barbara Rosberg show you how, step-by-step, in fun and creative dates.

GUARD YOUR HEART
ISBN 0-8423-5732-7

GUARDING LOVE (WORKBOOK)
ISBN 0-8423-7344-6

We all need to guard our hearts and marriages. It's only in a couples small group, among like-minded friends, that you can get the solid support you need to withstand attacks on your marriage. In *Guard Your Heart,* Gary and Barb Rosberg outline the unique dangers and temptations husbands and wives face. In the *Guarding Love* workbook, Gary and Barb Rosberg give you the tools to show your small group how to hold each other accountable to guarding their marriages—no matter what the cost.

Do you know of a marriage in your church or neighborhood that is vulnerable to attack? Start a small group for that couple with the *Guarding Love* workbook as a resource. Or invite that couple to a small group that is reading and applying this book and workbook. The workbook includes eight exciting group sessions and an easy-to-follow leader's guide.

**HEALING THE HURT IN YOUR MARRIAGE:
BEYOND CONFLICT TO FORGIVENESS**
ISBN 1-58997-104-3
Available Spring 2004

FORGIVING LOVE (WORKBOOK)
ISBN 0-8423-7491-4
Available Spring 2004

In *Healing the Hurt in Your Marriage: Beyond Conflict to Forgiveness,* Gary and Barbara Rosberg show you how to forgive past hurt in your marriage and close the loop on unresolved conflict. Restore an honest, whole relationship with your spouse. You probably know a dozen marriages that are deteriorating because one spouse is holding a grudge or because the husband and wife have never resolved their conflict, hurt, and anger. And most marriages have past hurts that are hindering the ongoing relationship. Gary and Barbara Rosberg show you how to break free of these past hurts and experience wholeness again. The most effective way to heal wounds is within the circle of encouraging believers who understand, know, and sympathize with you in the common struggles in marriage. The *Forgiving Love* workbook is perfect for small group members who can encourage each other to resolve conflict and start the healing process. Includes eight encouraging sessions and an easy-to-follow leader's guide.

RENEWING YOUR LOVE: Devotions for Couples
ISBN 0-8423-7346-2

Have the demands of everyday life pressed in on your marriage? Has your to-do list become more important than your relationship with your spouse? Is the TV the center of your home or the love you and your spouse share? This devotional from America's Family Coaches, Gary and Barb Rosberg, will help you and your spouse focus on your marriage, your relationship, and the love of your life. Let Gary and Barb guide you through thirty days of renewal and recommitment to your marriage by reviewing forgiving love, serving love, persevering love, guarding love, celebrating love, and renewing love through the lens of Scripture, reflection, prayer, and application.

Look for a persevering love book in the future from Gary and Barbara Rosberg and Tyndale House Publishers. This book will help you weather the storms of life without losing the passion for your spouse.

Also watch for a celebrating love book from your favorite family coaches, Gary and Barb Rosberg. This book will give you creative ideas on how to keep the fire and passion alive in your marriage.

Begin to divorce-proof your home, your church,
and your community today

Contact your local bookstore that sells
Christian books for all of the resources of
the Divorce-Proofing America's Marriages
campaign

or

call 888-ROSBERG (888-767-2374)

or

visit our Web site at

www.divorceproof.com.

MARRIAGE MAP
SELF-TESTS

$\mathcal{E}$ach self-test and checklist discussed in this book is included here in a format that is easy to photocopy for use by an individual couple or a small group of couples.

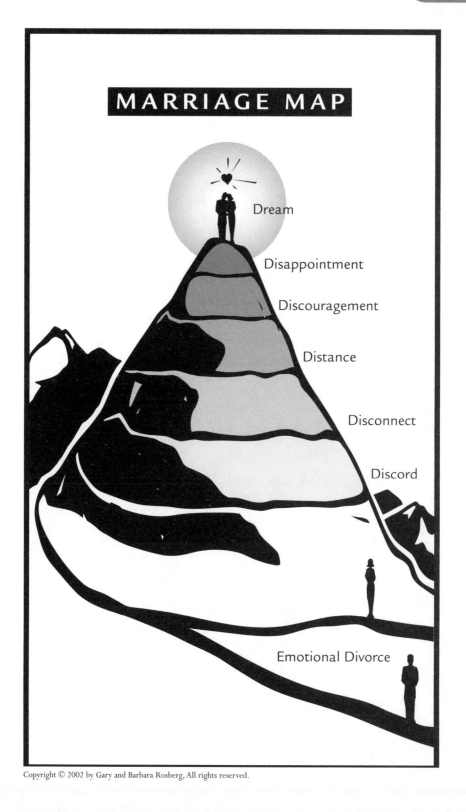

MARRIAGE MAP

Dream

Disappointment

Discouragement

Distance

Disconnect

Discord

Emotional Divorce

THE DREAM STOP

Compare yourself to these indicators, and check any that describe the current state of your marriage:

H	W	
❏	❏	I communicate freely with my spouse, and we keep no inappropriate secrets.
❏	❏	I forgive my spouse when I am wronged and seek forgiveness when I offend. I am loved without strings.
❏	❏	My spouse and I eagerly seek to discover and meet each other's needs.
❏	❏	We have faced and conquered difficult circumstances that have undone other marriages.
❏	❏	I consciously guard myself against threats and temptations that could pull our marriage apart.
❏	❏	We enjoy ongoing emotional, physical, and spiritual closeness.
❏	❏	We are committed to keeping our relationship fresh and alive "till death do us part."

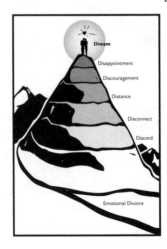

THE DISAPPOINTMENT STOP

Compare yourself to these indicators, and check any that describe the current state of your marriage:

H   W

❑   ❑   I have difficulty expressing affirmation to or about my spouse.

❑   ❑   My spouse isn't the flawless person I thought I married.

❑   ❑   I feel surprised and let down when I notice an imperfection in my spouse.

❑   ❑   My spouse and I have caused each other to feel hurt and angry.

❑   ❑   My spouse and I have experienced conflict over personality differences, male-female wiring, or ways of doing things we learned from our families.

❑   ❑   I compare my spouse to other people.

❑   ❑   I have a mental list of things I wish I could change about my spouse.

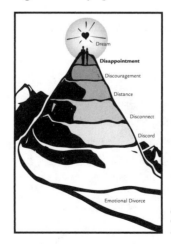

THE DISCOURAGEMENT STOP

Compare yourself to these indicators, and check any that describe the current state of your marriage:

H	W	
❑	❑	I often wonder if I am missing out on something in my marriage.
❑	❑	I have a mental list of reasons why I am dissatisfied with my marriage.
❑	❑	My spouse implies—or says—that I don't understand him or her or know how to meet his or her needs.
❑	❑	My own needs are not being met in my marriage. I feel as if my spouse's friends, work, church involvement, and/or the kids are more important than I am.
❑	❑	Even when I recognize my spouse's needs, I am not successful at meeting them.
❑	❑	I have a difficult time expressing my needs in a way my spouse can understand and act on.
❑	❑	I wonder if my choice of a spouse was a mistake.

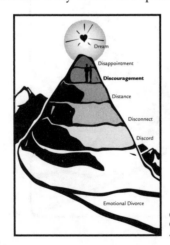

THE DISTANCE STOP

Compare yourself to these indicators, and check any that describe the current state of your marriage:

H **W**

❏ ❏ I could describe our relationship as "fair to partly cloudy, with no clearing in sight."

❏ ❏ I often fill my free time with activities that don't include my spouse.

❏ ❏ I have given up most of my expectations of my spouse.

❏ ❏ I wonder if my spouse ever feels excited about being married to me.

❏ ❏ My spouse sometimes seems like a stranger to me.

❏ ❏ I keep many of my thoughts and feelings from my spouse.

❏ ❏ I worry that we might someday face a problem bigger than our resolve to stay together.

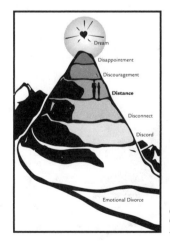

THE DISCONNECT STOP

Compare yourself to these indicators, and check any that describe the current state of your marriage:

H	W	
❏	❏	I sometimes feel lonely even when I'm with my spouse.
❏	❏	It is difficult for me to "feel" that my spouse loves me. I may know it intellectually, but I don't sense an emotional connection.
❏	❏	When we are together, we seldom have much to say to each other.
❏	❏	When we do talk to each other, we often misunderstand and misinterpret each other.
❏	❏	I prefer to devote my time, energy, and money to something or someone other than my spouse.
❏	❏	I doubt that my marriage can grow or change for the better.
❏	❏	I don't think my spouse is very interested in who I am or what I want to do.

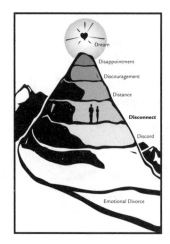

THE DISCORD STOP

Compare yourself to these indicators, and check any that describe the current state of your marriage:

H	W	
❏	❏	Most of my thoughts about my spouse are negative.
❏	❏	My spouse and I verbally lash out at each other, saying things that are hurtful.
❏	❏	I often wonder what it would be like not to be married—or to be married to a different person.
❏	❏	I daydream or fantasize about another person who would make a better spouse.
❏	❏	I feel as if my spouse and I are at war.
❏	❏	True tenderness with my spouse is a faded memory. We avoid sexual intimacy.
❏	❏	Family and close friends notice that our marriage is severely strained.

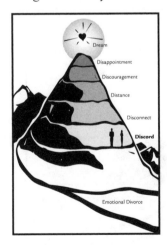

THE EMOTIONAL DIVORCE STOP

Compare yourself to these indicators, and check any that describe the current state of your marriage:

H	W	
❏	❏	I am staying married for some reason other than love for my spouse.
❏	❏	I have given up hope that my marriage could be better.
❏	❏	I pretend I'm okay with my marriage to keep up appearances.
❏	❏	My first goal in my marriage is to protect myself from further pain.
❏	❏	My spouse and I have separated or considered separating.
❏	❏	My heart is deeply attached to someone other than my spouse, even if I am not acting on that feeling.
❏	❏	I know I have already walked away from my marriage emotionally.

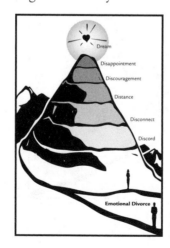

THE STATE OF OUR MARRIAGE

Review the seven stops on the marriage map as described below, then check one or two that you think most closely describe your marriage today. Realize that your spouse may have a different perspective on the state of your marriage. That being the case, Barb and I recommend that you both complete the exercise independently and then discuss your evaluation together. If it makes you feel too vulnerable to put your responses in the book, make two photocopies of the checklist and record your responses there.

H	W	
		DREAM
❏	❏	We communicate freely and keep no inappropriate secrets.
❏	❏	We forgive one another and seek forgiveness.
❏	❏	We seek to discover and meet each other's needs.
❏	❏	We face and conquer difficult circumstances.
❏	❏	We guard our marriage against threats and temptations.
❏	❏	We enjoy ongoing emotional, physical, and spiritual closeness.
❏	❏	We are committed "till death do us part."
		DISAPPOINTMENT
❏	❏	We have difficulty affirming each other.
❏	❏	We are surprised by each other's flaws.
❏	❏	We feel let down by each other's imperfections.
❏	❏	We cause each other hurt and anger.
❏	❏	We have conflict over our differences.
❏	❏	We compare each other to other people.
❏	❏	We wish we could change things in each other.

H	W	
		DISCOURAGEMENT
❑	❑	We often wonder if our marriage is missing something.
❑	❑	We have reasons to be dissatisfied with our marriage.
❑	❑	We don't understand each other or meet each other's needs.
❑	❑	We feel unimportant to each other.
❑	❑	We are not successful at meeting each other's needs.
❑	❑	We have difficulty expressing our needs to each other.
❑	❑	We wonder if we chose the wrong partner.
		DISTANCE
❑	❑	We do not see a letup in our difficulties.
❑	❑	We do many activities alone, without each other.
❑	❑	We have given up most expectations for each other.
❑	❑	We feel little excitement about being married to each other.
❑	❑	We sometimes feel and act like strangers.
❑	❑	We keep many of our thoughts and feelings from each other.
❑	❑	We face a problem that may eventually drive us apart.

H	W	
		DISCONNECT
❏	❏	We sometimes feel lonely even when we are together.
❏	❏	We don't feel an emotional connection to each other.
❏	❏	We seldom have much to say to each other.
❏	❏	We often misunderstand and misinterpret each other.
❏	❏	We direct our attention and activities away from each other.
❏	❏	We doubt that our marriage can change for the better.
❏	❏	We are not very interested in each other.
		DISCORD
❏	❏	We think and act negatively toward each other.
❏	❏	We lash out and hurt each other verbally.
❏	❏	We wonder what it would be like if we weren't married.
❏	❏	We wonder what it would be like to be married to someone else.
❏	❏	We feel that we are at war.
❏	❏	We lack tenderness and sexual intimacy.
❏	❏	We cannot hide from others that our marriage is severely strained.

H	W	
		EMOTIONAL DIVORCE
❑	❑	We are staying married for some reason other than love.
❑	❑	We have no hope that our marriage can be better.
❑	❑	We pretend that our marriage is okay to keep up appearances.
❑	❑	We only want to protect ourselves from further pain.
❑	❑	We have separated or have considered separating.
❑	❑	We are emotionally attached to someone else.
❑	❑	We have already walked away from our marriage emotionally.

GETTING BACK TO THE DREAM

Look at the list below, and check the loves that you feel will most effectively bring the growth your marriage needs. Then indicate in the blanks to the right which love you feel deserves the highest priority in your strategy to get back on the road to the dream. Identify your top three priorities. Complete the exercise independently, and then discuss your evaluation together. If it makes you feel too vulnerable to put your responses in the book, make two photocopies of the checklist and record your responses there.

H	W	
❑	❑	Forgiving love (priority: _____)
❑	❑	Serving love (priority: _____)
❑	❑	Persevering love (priority: _____)
❑	❑	Guarding love (priority: _____)
❑	❑	Celebrating love (priority: _____)
❑	❑	Renewing love (priority: _____)

OUR COVENANT HOME MARRIAGE CERTIFICATE

To the group leader:

On the following page is a copy of the "Our Covenant Home" certificate for you to give to each couple who completes this study. You can photocopy the certificate directly from the book. However, if you would like color versions of this certificate, you can download them from our Web site: www.divorceproof.com.

Our Covenant Home

Together as husband and wife, we declare our home a divorce-proofed home—a covenant home—built on the solid foundation of Jesus Christ, characterized by unconditional love, and devoted to our lifelong commitment to each other.

By signing this covenant, we promise to

- Initiate a forgiving love when we've offended each other or when conflict arises.
- Demonstrate serving love by putting each other's needs above our own.
- Exercise persevering love by walking through the most difficult times—hand in hand.
- Establish a guarding love that will safeguard our marriage and let no man, woman, or child divide us.
- Enjoy a celebrating love that keeps the spark alive in the relationship and celebrates you as my best friend.
- Experience a renewing love that says, "I'm committed to you until death do us part."

In the presence of God and these witnesses, and by a holy covenant, we promise to exhibit these loves toward each other every day. We promise that from this day forward, for better, for worse, for richer, for poorer, in sickness and in health, to forgive, to serve, to persevere, to guard, to celebrate, and to renew our love, forsaking all others as long as we both shall live.

_____
Husband's Signature

_____
Wife's Signature

WITNESSED THIS _____ DAY OF _____ , IN THE YEAR _____ BY _____

_____
Witness

_____
Witness

As for me and my house, we will serve the Lord.
—Joshua 24:15

DIVORCE-PROOFING CAMPAIGN AMERICA'S MARRIAGES

ABOUT THE AUTHORS

Dr. Gary and Barbara Rosberg are America's Family Coaches—equipping and encouraging America's families to live and finish life well. Having been married for nearly thirty years, Gary and Barbara have a unique message for couples.

They have committed the next decade of their ministry to divorce-proofing America's marriages. The cornerstone book in that campaign, *Divorce-Proof Your Marriage,* equips couples to strengthen their marriage to avoid the slide toward disconnection and emotional divorce. Other books the Rosbergs have written together include their Gold Medallion finalist and best-selling *The Five Love Needs of Men and Women,* as well as *40 Unforgettable Dates with Your Mate, Guard Your Heart,* and *Renewing Your Love,* a devotional for couples.

Together Gary and Barbara host a nationally syndicated, daily radio program, *America's Family Coaches . . . LIVE!* On this live call-in program heard in cities all across the country, they coach callers on many family-related issues. The Rosbergs also host a Saturday radio program on the award-winning secular WHO radio.

The Rosbergs have conducted conferences on family and relationship issues in more than a hundred cities across the country. Their flagship conference, Discover the Love of Your Life . . . All Over Again is impacting churches and communities nationwide. They are on the national speaking teams for Family Life's Weekend to Remember conference and "I Still Do" arena events for couples. Gary also has spoken to thousands of men at Promise Keepers stadium events annually since 1996 and to parents and adolescents at Focus on the Family "Life on the Edge" tour.

Gary, who earned his Ed. D. at Drake University, has been a marriage and family counselor for twenty years. He coaches Cross Trainers, a city-wide ministry that meets weekly with more than 600 men.

Barbara, in addition to writing many books with Gary, has written *Connecting with Your Wife.* She is also a featured speaker for the Extraordinary Women video series produced by the American Association of Christian Counselors.

The Rosbergs live outside Des Moines, Iowa, and are the parents of two adult daughters: Sarah, who lives near Des Moines with her husband, Scott, and their son, Mason; and Missy, a 2003 college graduate with a degree in communications.

For more information on the
Divorce-Proofing America's Marriages
campaign, contact:

America's Family Coaches
2540 105th Street, Suite 101
Des Moines, Iowa 50322
1-888-ROSBERG
www.divorceproof.com

Tune In to
America's Family Coaches . . . LIVE!

Listen every weekday for strong coaching on all your marriage, family, and relationship questions. On this interactive, call-in broadcast, Gary and Barbara Rosberg tackle real-life issues by coaching callers on what matters most in life—relationships. Tune in and be encouraged by America's leading family coaches.

For a listing of radio stations broadcasting
America's Family Coaches . . . LIVE!
call 1-888-ROSBERG
or
visit our Web site at www.afclive.com.